Strategic Foresight

Strategic Foresight

Accelerating Technological Change

Edited by
Sarah Lai-Yin Cheah

DE GRUYTER

ISBN 978-3-11-067290-9
e-ISBN (PDF) 978-3-11-067291-6
e-ISBN (EPUB) 978-3-11-067292-3

Library of Congress Control Number: 2020931960

Bibliographic information published by the Deutsche Nationalbibliothek
The Deutsche Nationalbibliothek lists this publication in the Deutsche Nationalbibliografie;
detailed bibliographic data are available on the Internet at http://dnb.dnb.de.

© 2020 Walter de Gruyter GmbH, Berlin/Boston
Cover image: akindo/DigitalVision Vectors/gettyimages.com
Typesetting: Integra Software Services Pvt. Ltd.
Printing and Binding: CPI books GmbH, Leck

www.degruyter.com

Foreword

Against the backdrop of rising trade tensions and slowing economic growth world-wide, the public policymakers of many countries have to grapple with increasingly complex issues ranging from ageing population to rising healthcare costs. Meanwhile, industries struggle to keep up with technological advances (e.g. robotics, internet of things, artificial intelligence and big data) to embrace the fourth industrial revolution (Industry 4.0).

The need for strategic foresight has never been so critical. Strategic foresight is a discipline comprising methods and tools that enable leaders and managers to broaden their perceptions of what and how the future possibilities may unfold, so as to identify and evaluate the various strategic options for decision making and resource mobilization to achieve the medium- to long-term vision. Institutes of higher learning and educators are expected to play a role in building the strategic foresight capability in the public and private sectors, thereby contributing to the national innovative capacity.

This book provides a good overview of strategic foresight discipline and the development of systemic foresight methodology (SFM) as a conceptual framework for designing and implementing foresight activities across multiple phases, while recognizing the interdependencies among multiple stakeholders, events and processes. Using a case-based approach, this book is written in a storytelling fashion that describes how the National Robotics R&D Programme Office of Singapore applies a range of foresight methods such as horizon scanning to develop market insights about service robotics, literature and patent analysis to gather technology insight, scenario stories to assess future uncertainty and impact, as well as roadmapping and Delphi survey to generate and validate integrated robotics R&D roadmap.

This book complements existing foresight methods with tools from other disciplines such as customer discovery from strategy management and quality function deployment from engineering, to develop future commercialization strategy for the organization. Throughout the cases, the challenges encountered at each SFM phase are illustrated and the strategic responses highlighted to lend breadth and depth to readers' appreciation of the strategic foresight concept. With this book, the authors hope to empower the readers with the necessary knowledge and tools to foster the building of strategic foresight capability that is critical in preparing organizations for changes, and steering them toward the desired future.

I applaud the editor and authors for their contribution to the practice of strategic foresight and its effective application in the pertinent topic of service robotics.

Professor Goh Cher Hiang
Engineering Design Innovation Centre
Faculty of Engineering, National University of Singapore (NUS)

https://doi.org/10.1515/9783110672916-202

Consultant to Chief Executive
Singapore National Robotics Programme
Agency for Science, Technology and Research (A*STAR)

Director, Singapore's first Micro-satellite project (X-Sat)
(aka "Father of Singapore Micro-satellite")
Advisor, NUS first Nano-satellite (Galassia)
Former Distinguished Member of Technical Staff of DSO National Laboratories

Preface

As our business environment becomes increasingly regulated and disrupted at the same time, business leaders are confronted with unprecedented challenges. Under conditions of growing ambiguity and volatility, those who are able to anticipate the forces on their industry and harness the potential of the uncertainty more creatively than their competitors will gain strategic advantage. Louis Pasteur would be no stranger to this principle. The French microbiologist, renowned for his achievements in vaccination, microbial fermentation and pasteurization, famously said "fortune favors the prepared mind." Indeed, rather than leaving discoveries to chance, one should be well-prepared for future opportunities by working hard to anticipate them and acquire the necessary ability, knowledge and skills to identify and exploit the opportunities should they arise. Similarly, business leaders who have the ability to deduce the industry forces and interpret the course of future realities will be able to steer their organization to "catch the wave".

Using a series of cases, this book aims to describe how organizations assess the future and formulate strategic plans using a systemic foresight methodology (SFM). As a result, this book is about strategic foresight in action. By looking into the real-time activities undertaken by the various actors in the organizations, we help our readers to understand who constructed the future in what manner and under what conditions to develop and implement what kinds of policies and programs. Through the cases, the authors aim to flesh out real-life issues, activities, pitfalls and challenges that are usually hidden or omitted in reports or discussions.

The first case is about how a national research organization in Singapore has applied the foresight method of horizon scanning to identify market opportunities for the service robotics landscape for the next five to ten years. Based on the study findings, the healthcare and environment domains seemed promising for robotics development and deployment that would significantly enhance productivity and propel Singapore towards its Smart Nation Initiative. In healthcare, the potential of smart hospitals seemed immense, with autonomous robots performing a variety of tasks from cleaning and delivery to even surgical operations. These would not only solve the manpower shortage problem, but also address the escalating healthcare costs of the aging population. However, pursuing the wide range of robotic types in healthcare would mean greater funding for different robotic technologies. Should the organization focus on (a) logistic management and indoor professional cleaning application to achieve operational efficiency, (b) surgical robots for clinical excellence or (c) telemedicine and rehabilitative robots for patient centricity? This case would take the readers through the business dilemma, and present the various options available to the manager for decision-making. Through the case, the readers can appreciate the (a) importance of horizon scanning in intelligence gathering as the first phase of SFM, (b) challenges encountered in applying horizon scanning or other information retrieval and analysis processes, (c) current challenges that can

https://doi.org/10.1515/9783110672916-203

present future growth opportunities for organizations, as well as (d) perspective of a national policymaker and the interplay between macro-level national considerations and market-level drivers and technological capabilities.

Building on the market insight of the first case, the second case depicts how the national research organization proceeded to conduct technology insight using the foresight methods of literature review and patent analysis. This case seeks to illustrate the importance of literature review and patent analysis methods in the intelligence phase of SFM to identify the key technologies that are critical to organizational success. It highlights the challenges an organization faces in conducting technology insight and the possible responses that can be adopted to address them. The quality of technology can hugely and effectively impact an organization's future developments and activities, and set the tone for its journey forward. The case also demonstrates how technology insight can reveal possible areas of R&D collaboration between private firms and public research institutes to enable the firms' development of innovative capabilities that are critical for their competitive advantage.

In the third case, the national research organization developed scenario stories to assess the future impact of soft robotics in the society and develop their deployment roadmap in the healthcare and industrial inspection domains. To proceed, the organization contemplated two possible approaches. It could either adopt the grant-call approach or the bottom-up proposal method. The grant-call approach would solicit proposals from a wide community of research performers through the mechanism of a grant call or invitation to apply for a grant. This approach would give it the opportunity to evaluate and select the most suitable proposals from hopefully a wide pool of candidates, but at the risk of receiving proposals with competing technologies or research duplication. The bottom-up proposal method would identify and invite the most suitable researchers to form a research team that would then collectively develop a proposal that would be holistic and integrated to solve specific problems. Mulling over the two approaches, the organization had to decide which would be the most appropriate path to take. This case aims to highlight the (a) importance of the imagination phase of SFM to generate future visions and scenarios, (b) process of scenario development to chart the future directions of an organization and its related industries, (c) importance of identifying the relevant stakeholders and using the appropriate platforms to engage them so as to understand their perception and mental models, (d) purpose and usefulness of storytelling in developing future scenarios and capturing their impact and uncertainty, (e) a range of collaboration strategies that vary by participation level and hierarchy degree available for organizations to co-create future value, and (f) trade-offs of community participation and partnerships involved in co-creation.

Based on the findings from the first three phases of SFM, the fourth case describes how the national research organization combined the market and technology insights, together with scenario stories, to generate roadmaps in three key technology areas that it had made prior investments in. The organization went on to validate the roadmaps with a Delphi survey, which yielded insightful results on the relative national competence and societal impact of the three technology areas. Given limited time and resources, which technology area should the organization continue to fund, and which should it kill or put on hold? This case discusses the (a) challenges of technology management and the importance of the integration phase of SFM, (b) relevance of the interpretation phase of SFM and application of roadmapping method to formulate strategies, and (c) application of Delphi surveys to validate roadmaps and prioritize resource allocation for future roadmap implementation.

In the final case, the national research organization was presented with three possible options for commercializing its technology in the intervention phase of SFM. First, there was the option of licensing the intellectual property (IP), wherein the research institute owning the patent (a form of IP) could grant the commercial rights of the IP to an existing company in exchange for a fee and royalty. Second, the organization could consider R&D collaboration where the research institute owning the patent would collaborate with a partner organization to jointly develop the technology to improve its technology readiness level before commercializing it into products and services. The third possible pathway could be a spin-off, in which a member of the researcher team working on the technology would form a new, independent, legal entity to license the IP from the parent research institute for commercialization. Each of these three options had its merits and limitations. This case aims to illustrate the (a) relevance of customer discovery process in identifying potential customers, ascertaining product-market fit, as well as developing commercially viable business models, (b) utilization of multi-dimensional framework to assess the commercial potential of new product applications, and (c) importance of quality function deployment process to capture and map customer requirements into new product functionalities.

I hope that you will enjoy reading this book as much as I have enjoyed writing it.

Sarah Lai-Yin Cheah

Acknowledgements

I would like to express my gratitude to Prof Quek Tong Boon, Prof Goh Cher Hiang and Rayner Ng for the opportunity to work with the National Robotics R&D Programme Office of Singapore on the exciting task of developing robotics road-mapping and commercialization strategy for Singapore, as well as to Edmund Ooi for his support in contributing materials to the cases. My heartfelt thanks go to Ou Hai-Ling and Siddharth Kamani who have helped to review the cases. I would like to acknowledge Cameron Kheng and Li Shiyu for conducting initial research on the cases, and Kritesh Patel for assisting in interview transcripts before the authors can commence work on the cases and teaching resources. Finally, I would like to thank my husband Stephen and daughter Victoria for their love and support in the development of this book.

https://doi.org/10.1515/9783110672916-204

Contents

List of Figures

https://doi.org/10.1515/9783110672916-206

About the Editor

Dr Sarah Lai-Yin Cheah

Qualifications:
PhD, Business School, University of South Australia
MBA, Nanyang Business School, Nanyang Technological University
BEng (Electrical Engineering) (Honours), National University of Singapore

Profile description

Dr Sarah Cheah is Associate Professor with the NUS Business School, with research and practice in public-private research collaboration and technology transfer, intellectual property (IP) management, commercialization and spin-off. She lectures in Innovation, Entrepreneurship and Strategic Foresight in BBA and MBA programs She also taught in Management of Technological Innovation with the MBA and Technopreneurship Programs in 2003-2013, and MSc Business Analytics in 2013-2014. She has led consulting practicum and research studies on innovation with business federations, chambers of commerce and multi-national corporations (MNC). Dr Cheah is currently advisor on strategic foresight to the largest oil and gas company in Thailand. She provides executive training for corporations and public policymakers from Singapore, Indonesia, Thailand, Vietnam and China.

She was consultant to the National Robotics R&D Programme (NR2P) on robotics R&D roadmapping and commercialization strategy, the Agency for Science, Technology and Research (A*STAR) Institute of Materials Research and Engineering (IMRE) on technology road-mapping, A*ccelerate on diagnostics development ecosystem study, A*STAR Science and Engineering Research Council (SERC) on Futurescape 2025, and Reviewer with Singapore National Research Foundation (NRF)'s grant call for Science of Research, Innovation and Enterprise (SRIE). She provided consultancy to Venture Capital firm on new technology ventures and the Singapore Institute of Technology Lean Transformation Innovation Centre. She is Scientific Panel Member with The International Society for Professional Innovation Management (ISPIM).

Prior to joining NUS, Dr Cheah held the position of Vice President with A*STAR ETPL (former A*ccelerate), responsible for strategic planning, science and technology foresight and market analytics, to identify emerging technologies with commercial potential, and promote transfer of technology and knowledge from public research institutes to the industry. From her research work involving more than 1,000 companies, she has captured their insights as journal articles and teaching cases, published with Taylor and Francis, Pearson Education, Cengage Learning Asia and Ivey Publishing.

https://doi.org/10.1515/9783110672916-207

List of Contributors

Sarah Lai-Yin Cheah is an Associate Professor with the Department of Management and Organization in the Business School of the National University of Singapore.

Ozcan Saritas is Professor, Head of Laboratory for Science and Technology Studies, Institute for Statistical Studies and Economics of Knowledge, National Research University Higher School of Economics, Moscow, Russian Federation.

Saiteja Pattalachinti just graduated with Bachelor of Technology at the National Institute of Technology Tiruchirappalli.

https://doi.org/10.1515/9783110672916-208

Sarah Cheah
1 Introduction

As companies and organizations are forced to transform in response to social, technological, economic and political changes, it is important for business leaders and managers to acquire knowledge and skills in foresight methods to competitively identify new opportunities and set an appropriate direction for the mid- to long-term time horizon. Their ability to interpret weak signals and anticipate future trends in technology and market are critical in preparing the organization for the new uncertainty ahead. Success and advantage go to those who are best at deducing the forces acting on their sector, and who are best at anticipating and adapting to avoid threats and act on opportunities.

Strategic foresight is discipline that organizations should adopt to gather, interpret and manage information about the future environment they plan to operate in. This book introduces the concept of strategic foresight and advocates a holistic and systemic foresight methodology (SFM) that is suitable for organizations in the public and private sectors. The SFM approach comprises six phases: intelligence, imagination, integration, interpretation, intervention and impact. Using real-life cases as practical examples, the book demonstrates how organizations can apply a range of foresight methods and resources across the first five phases to (a) perform horizon scanning for market insight and technology forecast in the intelligence phase, (b) develop scenarios in the imagination phase, (c) leverage expert networks to analyze investment priorities in the integration phase, (d) generate roadmaps in the interpretation phase, and (e) formulate R&D plans and commercialization strategy in the intervention phase.

This book aims to provide overview of the SFM to enable organizations to identify critical technologies and new opportunities for long-term growth. It articulates the importance of strategic foresight and its contribution to an organization's success. The authors explain lucidly the strategies that can assist in a complex business environment and introduce tools to help address future scenarios. Robust and proven strategies are discussed with case studies, allowing the readers to gain a better insight into how the strategies can be implemented pragmatically. The authors not only trace the journey of organizations in conducting foresight through the various phases to flesh out real-life issues, but also introduce the latest management thinking and tools on foresight in strategic business decision.

This book is organized into eight chapters, with the first chapter on introduction. The second chapter provides an overview of SFM. The remaining five chapters cover one case each using a storytelling approach, before ending with recommended readings on the relevant foresight method and conceptual frameworks, as well as proposed review and discussion questions for readers to enable deeper

https://doi.org/10.1515/9783110672916-001

analysis. In the final chapter, the book is concluded with several themes and implications distilled from the cases.

The Chapter 2 on Systemic Foresight Methodology in Action by Ozcan Saritas and Sarah Cheah provides an introduction to strategic foresight. It gives an overview of the discipline as well as the emergence and development of SFM. It introduces the current conceptual frameworks of SFM. Rather than focusing on a particular method, the SFM recognizes the need for a collection of complementary methods that organizations can use to guide them through its six phases. This chapter will provide an overview of the various tools and techniques that business leaders and managers may adopt in each phase. In the first phase of intelligence, methods such as horizon scanning, social network analysis, knowledge/research maps, literature review, text/data mining and patent analysis have been adopted by the public and private sector organizations. These methods provide the basic input to the next phase of imagination phase, where one or more of the following tools may be employed: scenario stories, gaming, visioning, agent-based modeling, scenario modeling and system dynamics. During the imagination phase, creative generation of ideas and information about the future takes place. These have to be then analyzed and assessed for their relative risks and benefits in the third phase of integration, where the typical techniques comprise backcasting, Delphi survey, multi-criteria analysis, risk assessment and cost-benefit analysis. Following the decision on the most desirable and preferable future, the interpretation phase aims to connect this future with the present and sets out agenda and strategies for action, employing methods ranging from roadmapping and strategic planning to logic framework and linear programming. The strategic plans generated will be used as input in the next phase of intervention to create and impact policies and action plans using processes such as customer discovery and quality function deployment. In the final impact phase, it is important to review and evaluate the impact contributed by the output of the preceding phases using methods such as interviews and surveys on impacted stakeholders to gather new knowledge and gain insight that can be provided as feedback learning into the start of the next SFM cycle.

The Chapter 3 on Market Insight: Horizon Scanning of Service Robotics Landscape by Sarah Cheah is the first of a five-case series depicting the SFM that organizations generally use to gather information about future scenarios of their operating environment and formulating long-term strategies to address them. The case focuses on the first phase of intelligence, where the National Robotics Program (NRP) Office of Singapore applied the foresight technique of horizon scanning to identify market drivers, key business sectors and applications in service robotics for the country. The research team has just completed a horizon scanning study that identified two domains – healthcare and environment – as possible targets to deploy robotics technological solutions. The suitability of the technologies to be funded would be evaluated in three aspects: (a) ability to meet national needs, (b) ability to solve manpower shortage and (c) ability to address aging population issues.

The Chapter 4 on Technology Insight: Literature Review and Patent Analysis of Service Robot Research by Sarah Cheah is the second of the SFM case series that illustrates how organizations identify key technologies that are critical to organizational success. The case focuses on the first phase of SFM – intelligence phase – where the NRP has applied the foresight techniques of literature review and patent analysis to conduct technology insight. Patent data would provide valuable technical information that could be used to plot the growth trajectory of technologies over time. One of the areas that had kept the team busy was the Modular Self-Reconfigurable Robots (MSRR) research project that had seen the spin-off of LionsBot International Pte Ltd. The young company aimed to incorporate MSRR technology to provide cleaning robots as a service for commercial, industrial and public spaces in Singapore by 2019. While the team was heartened by the interest in LionsBot's cleaning robots among local cleaning companies, they wondered if the value of underlying MSRR technology could be further enhanced by the young company's organic growth or its collaboration with a strong player in the related technology domain.

The Chapter 5 on Assessing Future Impact: Developing Scenario Stories by Sarah Cheah is the third of the five-case SFM series depicting the imagination phase where organizations imagine scenarios of their future operating environment with the view to identifying and developing capabilities to leverage opportunities presented in the scenarios. In 2017, the NRP held a series of workshops with the scientific and business community. These inter-disciplinary workshops aimed to encourage participation from diverse industries to articulate their perception of possible futures with soft robotics in society, communicate their visions of tomorrow as a form of storytelling, and develop them into narrative scenarios. The scenario stories served to promote awareness of future societal trends and disseminate knowledge about robotic technologies and their socio-economic impact, with the view to increasing social acceptance of future robotics deployment across the industries. From the workshop sessions, several narratives had emerged. In the healthcare domain, scenario stories revolved around assistive and surgical devices, as well as wearables for possible deployment in the near future. The mental pictures articulated by the participants for the industrial inspection domain dwelled on flexible structures like snake robots that could conduct an inspection in highly complex mechanical systems. Drawing upon these scenario stories as inspiration, the team began to make plans to develop future robotics R&D and commercialization roadmap for various industries.

The Chapter 6 on Technology Management: Building and Validating Roadmaps by Sarah Cheah is the fourth of the five-case series depicting the integration and interpretation phases. The integration phase focuses on analyzing and prioritizing investment options using techniques such as Delphi that generates consensus on priorities among experts. The interpretation phase develops strategy using methods such as roadmapping. Having completed the earlier three phases of SFM, the NRP team had generated technology/R&D roadmaps in three key areas: (a) robotic end-effectors with integrated perception (or gripper robotics), (b) autonomous vehicles with sensor fusion and (c) on-chip Light Detection and Ranging (LiDAR) system for autonomous robotics. Building on these technology/R&D roadmaps, integrated roadmaps were also developed for two target domains: healthcare and environment. The project team went on to validate these roadmaps through a Delphi survey involving 70 industry and technology experts. The survey had several findings. First, in line with expectations, autonomous vehicles were found to have the greatest impact for social and citizen well-being, while LiDAR and gripper robotics had a great impact for industry and economic growth. Second, as the team had postulated, Singapore's strongest competence in gripper robotics, LiDAR and autonomous vehicles was evident in its availability of funding, infrastructure and design/engineering know-how, respectively. Third, LiDAR and autonomous vehicles were found to have similar forecasted realization as anticipated due to their complementarity with each other. However, widespread use for gripper robotics was projected to take a longer time than that of LiDAR and autonomous vehicles, which went counter to the NRP team's understanding that the latter would take a longer time due to the more stringent safety regulations imposed by the local land transport authority.

The Chapter 7 on Commercialization Strategy with Quality Function Deployment by Sarah Cheah and Saiteja Pattalachinti is the last of the five-case series depicting the final SFM phase, intervention phase, where organizations develop R&D plans and commercialization pathways to create and capture future value. The NRP was presented with a project that involved the development of end-effector technology integrated with computer vision. End-effectors or grippers referred to the last link of a robot that was designed to interact with the environment, such as picking and placing objects at specific locations. They were mainly used for industrial purposes to pick and place standard-sized objects in a controlled environment. They were also used to perform precision surgeries as part of surgical robots. With advances in emerging technologies such as artificial intelligence (AI), tactile sensing, machine learning and computer vision, the functions of a gripper could be significantly enhanced by incorporating them to guide its grasping strategy. The gripper technology with computer vision would stand out in a market flooded with grippers that could only handle pre-determined standard-sized objects that lacked flexibility and sensing ability to work in a complex environment. The NRP team had to choose a commercialization pathway that would be the best option for the gripper technology with computer vision.

In conclusion, through the real-life cases, this book highlights the challenges of conducting foresight in various stages, the range of foresight tools and resources available to formulate strategies to address the volatility, uncertainty, complexity and ambiguity of the future operating environment. This book aims to become a milestone in furthering the concepts of foresight and strategic management.

Ozcan Saritas and Sarah Cheah

2 Systemic Foresight Methodology in Action

The emergence and development of SFM

Background

Recent decades have witnessed increasing complexities in societies. The world has got better for some. However, the vast majority still suffers from social and economic instability and hostility due to limited access to food, energy and water, economic recession, climate change, conflicts, and respective migration. The new global context suggests a more interconnected and interdependent world with increased flow of finance and investment as well as information and human connectivity. This transformation is accelerated by rapid technological progress in areas such as information and communication technologies (ICTs), artificial intelligence (AI) and robotics, bio- and nano-technologies, and advanced production technologies among the others. The new ICT enabled and networked societal demands of inclusiveness and equity through freedom of association and expression with full protection of human rights. There is now an emerging need for new international regulations and standards to govern trade, quality, labor, environment and intellectual property rights (Saritas, 2010a), and novel ways of thinking about the future in a more complex and uncertain world.

Institutional foresight has been evolving since the early 1950s. The practice of foresight has evolved since then with the changing world situations as well as the development of the foresight theory itself in response to those changes (Saritas, 2013). One of the widely accepted definitions of foresight still remains valid to a large extent: "a systematic, participatory, future intelligence-gathering and medium- to long-term vision building process aimed at enabling present-day decisions and mobilizing joint action" (Miles and Keenan, 2002). However, due to the aforementioned transformations in the global context and technological advancements, new and more systemic approaches are required. Observing this necessity, the systemic foresight methodology (SFM) has been developed as a response to increasing complexity and uncertainty of the future, with the aim of proposing a conceptual framework for designing and implementing foresight activities. The key premises of the SFM are established on the concept of systems thinking (Saritas,

Note: The contributions by Dr. Ozcan Saritas in this publication were supported within the framework of the Basic Research Program at the National Research University Higher School of Economics (HSE) and were funded within the framework of the subsidy granted to the HSE by the Government of the Russian Federation for the implementation of the Global Competitiveness Program.

https://doi.org/10.1515/9783110672916-002

2006). The SFM considers situations by recognizing the interconnections and inter-dependencies between different events, actors and processes. The holistic view of the events suggests that political, economic, social, technological, ecological and legal (PESTEL) systems co-exist and are inter-linked in cascaded systems of governance from global to international, national to regional, and sectoral to thematic levels. Actors within these systems are networked with each other, and their systemic and synchronized action is needed to achieve any successful change process while meeting the expectations of the stakeholders with power, urgency and legitimacy.

This chapter aims at giving a brief description of SFM with a stocktaking of earlier work, which led to the development and further advancement of the SFM methodology process. Examples of practice are given with case studies, and future prospects for the development of SFM are discussed with new and emerging technologies. The chapter ends with a description of how SFM was made use of as a methodology of the studies undertaken within the scope of this book.

Systemic foresight methodology: Process and phases

The process of the SFM is also systemic in that the proposed methodology brings together divergent and convergent methods with exploratory, normative and action-oriented thinking. The process is represented with 7+1 "I"s. The first seven "I"s represent the flow of the process with a set of consecutive steps, while the eighth "I" represents the participatory character of foresight:
(a) Initiation (Scoping)
(b) Intelligence (Scanning)
(c) Imagination (Scenarios)
(d) Integration (Setting priorities)
(e) Interpretation (Strategies)
(f) Implementation (Actions)
(g) Impact (Evaluation) with a continuous
(h) Interaction (Inclusivity) across the process

The SFM process can be viewed as a series of phases. The consecutive phases aim at investigating how systems (whether human and social systems, or industrial and innovation systems) are understood, approached and intervened for a successful change program. The phases are iterative and can be repeated as many times until the practitioners come to conclusion that their complete function has been fulfilled.

Briefly, the **Initiation** phase of SFM is concerned with the scoping of the foresight exercise. Major decisions are made on the scope and coverage of the activity. This phase examines the goals and specific objectives of the activity, its scope and coverage, intended uses and users of its outputs and outcomes. Initiation is critical as the boundaries of the foresight exercise are determined in this phase. Therefore, this can also be considered as an initial prioritization stage. Decisions on the process and methodology of the exercise, stakeholders to be engaged, key milestones, deliverables and dissemination activities are also made at this stage.

Following the Initiation phase, the actual SFM process begins with the **Intelligence** phase. This may also be considered as the scanning and surveying phase. The aim of this phase is to attain a comprehensive analysis of systems and situations the foresight exercise is concerned with. Foresight activities usually deal with complex systems with a large number of interacting elements. Both environmental and horizon scanning activities are conducted to understand trends, drivers of change, weak signals of emerging developments, wild cards/surprises/ shocks, and discontinuities (Saritas and Smith, 2011). A PESTEL framework is commonly used to scan a wide variety of issues in political, economic, social, technological, environmental and legal systems. This phase typically identifies and prioritizes important issues and uncertainties, which will shape the future.

Imagination is the creative and innovative phase of SFM where future-oriented divergent thinking is applied to explore alternative futures. Unlike future prediction and forecasting, foresight is concerned with exploring alternative futures and developing normative visions and priorities. The input generated from the Intelligence phase is synthesized as future narratives in the form of scenarios and models of the future. These give more complete and systemic picture of the future by showing the interplay between different systems and their elements. Qualitative and quantitative methods such as scenario planning, modelling, gaming, system dynamics and simulation are used to help explore alternative futures and make assessments of their impacts. Use of weak signals and wild cards from the Intelligence phase may help to test the adaptive capacity of systems under extreme conditions, surprises and shocks.

Integration is the phase where alternative futures are appraised, normative visions are articulated, and priorities are identified. This process involves a thorough analysis of the scenarios and models developed in the previous phase. This is a multifaceted process, where claims of different stakeholders must be considered adequately to make sure that future systems designed are resilient in the long term. The end product of this phase is an agreed model of the future, which will imply the targets to be achieved within the time horizon set for the foresight activity.

The **Interpretation** phase is primarily considered as the strategy phase. The earlier phases of SFM discussed extensively the question of "where we are" at the Intelligence phase. Then during the Imagination and Integration phases the question of "where we want to go" was answered. Hence, the Interpretation phase has the function of filling the gap between where we are and where we want to go, with a question of "how to get there". The gap between the future and the present is filled in this phase by suggesting transitions and transformations needed in the long, medium and short terms. Thus, this phase represents a more "convergent" phase. The outputs of this phase are usually expected to be in the form of strategic roadmaps.

Foresight exercises are expected to inform policies and actions. Therefore, the **Intervention** phase of the SFM is concerned with the actions, where formulated priorities, strategies and follow-up steps are outlined and communicated with the key actors and stakeholders. The aim is to inform present day decisions concerning immediate change actions to begin structural and behavioral transformations as well as to influence and shape wider contexts to add value for the viability and development of systems.

Impact is the phase where foresight is evaluated and embedded to understand the extent the activity has achieved its objectives, the impact generated and the extended activities that should be laid out to move forward. Foresight process requires substantive investments, often through public funding, and implies considerable costs in terms of time, logistics and human resources. If impacts of foresight cannot be made clear throughout the activity, the commitment for dedicating resources will decrease, and as a result, the activity will be discontinued. This phase examines the impacts of foresight during the process of implementation (e.g. production of baseline reports, articulation of visions, and building new linkages), immediately after the completion of the activity (e.g. new integrated projects and programs), and sometime later (e.g. innovation impacts and new working communities).

Interaction is one of the main distinguishing features of foresight from other long range planning activities as the activity is inclusive and participative. Different from the other phases, Interaction should be observed throughout the foresight process. A thorough stakeholder analysis is important for any foresight exercise to make sure that all legitimate viewpoints are reflected in the process. The SFM recognizes the inclusiveness and equity through freedom of association and expression and the role of the democratic society. This phase emphasizes the need for effectiveness and efficiency in meeting the stakeholders' expectations and sustainable use of resources, and therefore, aims to develop mechanisms to provide engagement of system actors ranging from policy makers to industry, research to higher education, as well as associations and NGOs among the others.

The overall SFM process and phases draw upon a variety of qualitative and quantitative methods, and their integrated use. Whether quantitative or qualitative, methods are not departure points of SFM. Suitable methods are combined in line with the context and content of the foresight exercise as well as available resources to constitute a full foresight methodology. The overall methodology aims at developing and supporting understanding of situations in their temporal nature, enabling divergent thinking within a defined time horizon, prioritizing issues and setting up visions, as well as converging those visions into policies and strategies. Certain methods during the process help to enable networking, mutual learning, collective visioning and action-oriented thinking.

Practical applications of SFM

SFM has been developed since the initial launch of the idea in Saritas (2006). Entitled as "Systems Thinking for Foresight", this Ph.D. thesis set the key principles of SFM based on the ideas of systems theory and a critical review of the evolution of foresight practice. SFM constituted a background and main methodological approach to the ForSTI (Foresight for Science, Technology and Innovation) activities described by Miles, Saritas and Sokolov (2016). During its process of development, a number of studies have made use of the SFM methodology on a wide variety of topics. Some of the recent cases, which made use of the SFM as an overall methodological approach, are as follows:

Case 1:   Future of Higher Education in Romania. One of the earliest full-scale applications of SFM was in the scope of the project entitled "Quality and Leadership for Romanian Higher Education". The primary purpose of the project was to help generate or enhance the scientific and educational capacity of Romanian universities to be prepared for the opportunities and challenges of the twenty first century. The SFM methodology was fully described by Saritas (2010b) in "The For-Uni Blueprint for Organizing Foresight in Universities" (Curaj, 2010) and implemented during the actual foresight exercise. Among the key outputs of the project were visions and strategies for Romanian higher education towards 2025.

Case 2:   Reinventing product-service systems: the case of Singapore. A foresight study was conducted by the national R&D agency of Singapore to help science and technology decision makers identify key capability areas of R&D investment to support the manufacturing industry's growth in the country and the region. Within the scope of this study, SFM was adopted as a foresight approach to identify core areas to be developed to support the country's future growth of product-service systems (Cheah, Yang and Saritas, 2019).

Case 3:   A foresight exercise was undertaken to identify science, technology and innovation (STI) priorities for South Africa towards 2030. The study aimed at contributing to the following STI objectives of the country, including advancing the capacity of the national innovation system to contribute to socio-economic development; and enhancing South Africa's capacity for generating knowledge to produce world class research outputs, as well as innovative products and processes thereafter. The foresight study represented a fully-fledged application of the SFM methodology, with big data-based horizon scanning, scenario planning, priority setting and strategy formulation. Bibliometric and semantic analysis methods were used as key methods. The bibliometric analysis helped to understand South Africa's competences in research with key STI focus areas, scientific capacity within the country and key collaborators across the world and in

Africa. The temporal analysis of scientific outputs indicated the mature and emerging areas in South African research landscape. The semantic analysis helped to investigate each priority domain through large datasets consisting of scientific articles, patents, news, grants and analytical reports to describe emerging issues and topics. The results of the analysis were provided in the report with detailed interpretations.

Case 4: The foresight project on the "Digitalization of Russia" aimed at exploring the digitalization trends in Russia with a three- to five-year perspective. Drawing mainly on the Intelligence phase, the project scanned main strategies and initiatives by the government, state-owned and private companies, and research organizations with their impacts on the country's social, technological and economic development. This allowed providing a bird's eye view of the state of digitalization in Russia. In cooperation with Business Finland, the project also made a benchmark of Russia with Finland, as one of the leading countries in the era of digitalization. The big data analytics method helped to provide understanding of the current landscape of digitalization in both countries by looking at scientific publications and media resources. This benchmark also helped to show the opportunities for collaboration. The scanning study was taken forward with the case examples of the companies adopting digital technologies (e.g. blockchain, augmented reality (AR), virtual reality (VR), big data) in the health, energy and transport sectors.

Case 5: One of the most recent applications of SFM was for "Domestic Military Disaster Mitigation in Canada" (Saul, 2019). Applying SFM, the study examined the potential policy implications of the employment of military assets to address gaps in municipal and provincial capability of disaster management. The study formulates policy recommendations for future military and public safety applications. Four phases of SFM were used in particular within the context of the study, including Intelligence, Imagination, Integration and Interpretation. Applying SFM, the study specifically examined prudent external and internal drivers associated with Canadian disaster and emergency management and the use of Canadian Armed Forces (CAF). The study concluded that a paradigm shift is needed to prioritize mitigation and preparedness over response and recovery. To address increasing disaster costs, it is recommended that Canada should consider a fundamental transition in the employment of the CAF.

Future prospects for further advancement of the SFM

The variety of methods used for foresight keeps expanding (Saritas and Burmaoglu, 2015). One of the future prospects for SFM is to make use of these new methods, tools and techniques, and methodologies with their new combinations to respond to changing contexts and contents of foresight. Following the advancements in comput-ing technologies – both in hardware with more data storage and processing capabil-ity; and software with new algorithms for data analytics and machine-learning technologies, the SFM continuously strives for making use of big data, as new evi-dence base for foresight (Daim, Chiavetta, Porter and Saritas, 2016).

Some of the earlier work made use of network analysis as a systemic tool for interrelatedness and interdependencies of the issues and actors within foresight process (Nugroho and Saritas, 2009). Later, a temporal dimension was added into the process with the introduction of the evolutionary scenario process, which sup-ported to Imagination phase of SFM (Saritas and Nugroho, 2012).

More recent work demonstrated various ways of using big data for SFM to iden-tify trends, weak signals and wild cards. This work can be grouped under three cat-egories. The first group is concerned with the monitoring and evolution of theory in various scientific fields. The second group is dedicated to the development and demonstration of the more advanced SFM process with the use of new computing technologies. Finally, the third group focuses on the use of SFM in different the-matic and sectoral areas with the use of big data.

Concerning the first group, Saritas and Burmaoglu (2015) used a scientometric analysis of publications on foresight (in other words Future-oriented Technology Analysis (FTA)) to explore trends in the evolution of quantitative, qualitative and semi-quantitative foresight methods. More recent work by Burmaoglu and Saritas (2019) examined the evolution of the Innovation Policy theory and discussed the emergence of new trends in the field by arguing if these new trends can be inter-preted as signals of a paradigm shift in the field.

Regarding the development of more advanced process for SFM, Ena, Mikova, Saritas and Sokolov (2016) developed a methodology for monitoring trends in the Intelligence phase with the use of semantic technologies. This process was later ad-vanced with the combination of dynamic term clustering and semantic analysis to identify developing trends, stabilized and declining trends, weak signals of emerg-ing trends as well as wild cards (Bakhtin and Saritas, 2016). In a more recent work, Bakhtin, Saritas, Chulok, Kuzminov and Timofeev (2017) indicate how science and strategy affect each other by comparing and contrasting future-oriented work, such as strategy and policy documents, with scientific work such as papers, patents and conferences. This study links future priorities with practical scientific work on site.

The final category involves studies on the demonstration of SFM with more ad-vanced computational methods. Saritas and Burmaoglu (2016) and Burmaoglu and Saritas (2017) used scientometric analysis in combination with patent analysis for identifying trends (Intelligence), developing future scenarios (Imagination), identi-fying priorities (Integration), developing strategic roadmaps (Interpretation), and identifying actions in the domain of military R&D and energy fields. Saritas and Kuzminov (2017) identified global challenges and trends in agriculture and discussed the impacts of this scanning work for the formulation of strategies for successful adaptation and mitigation. Burmaoglu, Saritas, Kidak and Camuz (2017) showed the evolution of the connected health concept through a scientometric analysis and combined this approach with a network analysis. Similarly, Aydogdu, Burmaoglu, Saritas and Cakir (2017) demonstrated the use of a scientometric analysis in the Intelligence phase with the use of strategic roadmaps in the Interpretation and Impact phases by examining the use of nanotechnology in the defense industry.

Ongoing work explores the use of more advanced technologies for SFM. Artificial Intelligence and other newly emerging and evolving technologies give first signals of the next-generation of foresight, which will be characterized by human-technology interaction and creativity. In this respect, it is expected that all phases of the SFM process will be affected by the use of advanced analytics, Artificial Intelligence, human-machine systems, artificial and virtual reality technologies, robotics, new production technologies and social networks as well as blockchain technologies. Burmaoglu and Saritas (2020) describe the use of Blockchain for Foresight, and Science and Technology Policy making, and introduce the concept of "Ideachain". How foresight is becoming a platform for converging technologies and what new approaches are expected to emerge for SFM are extensively discussed by the incoming work of Saritas (2020).

The use of SFM in strategic foresight

This section describes how SFM was used as a methodological approach for the studies included in this book. The five case studies presented in Chapter 3 to Chapter 7 draw upon the SFM process from Intelligence to Impact phases. Among the methods mapped under each phase of SFM in Table 2.1, those with asterisks were used in the studies undertaken.

This section highlights the definition and applications of various foresight methods across the phases, particularly those that have been adopted in the cases of this book.

Horizon scanning

Horizon scanning refers to the systematic search for prevalent trends, threats and opportunities that had the potential to affect the likelihood of meeting organizational goals (Sutherland et al., 2010). It has become increasingly prevalent in recent years by organizations that aim to anticipate issues, and gather information and knowledge about them to support them in decision making. For example, the Health Policy Advisory Committee on Technology (HealthPACT) that was created in 2003,

Table 2.1: SFM in strategic foresight.

Systemic Foresight Methodology (SFM)					
Intelligence	**Imagination**	**Integration**	**Interpretation**	**Intervention**	**Impact**
– Horizon scan*	– Scenario stories*	– Delphi survey*	– Roadmapping*	– Customer discovery*	– Interview
– Literature review*	– Scenario modeling	– Backcasting	– SWOT analysis	– Quality function deployment*	– Survey
– Patent analysis*	– Gaming	– Multi-criteria analysis	– Strategic planning	– R&D planning	– Policy review
– Text/data mining	– Visioning	– Risk assessment	– Cross-impact analysis	– Action planning	– Impact indicator development
– Social network analysis	– Agent-based modeling	– Cost-benefit analysis	– Logic framework	– Communication planning	– Policy impact assessment
– Knowledge/ research map	– System dynamics		– Linear programming		

Source: Cheah et al. (2018)

comprising the Australian state and territory health department representatives, conducted horizon scanning of the grey and peer-reviewed literature to identify new and emerging practices that may affect the public health systems of Australia and New Zealand. From their horizon scanning processes, they have identified not only high-performance targets for investment, but also low-performance targets for disinvestment, to optimize the use of national healthcare budget. In 2013, HealthPACT's horizon scanning results revealed that the increasingly popular platelet-rich plasma (PRP) for the treatment of knee osteoarthritis was actually poor compared with the current nonsteroidal anti-inflammatory drugs (NSAID) treatment and has since been stopped from using public funding for treatment (Mundy, 2017).

In Chapter 3, a Singapore public agency advancing robotics solutions used the horizon scanning approach to identify two domains – healthcare and environment – as possible targets to deploy robotics technological solutions.

Literature review

Literature review is the process of identifying, evaluating, and interpreting the existing body of recorded documents (Fink, 2019). Prior to exploring a new research area, literature review is usually conducted to establish direction for the field of the topic or define the scope of research activity. It is motivated by the attempt to avoid "reinventing the wheel" and build on the existing body of knowledge. However, when the nature of research topic is unclear, it is challenging to delineate the boundaries for the research activity. The approach generally involves four key aspects:
(a) definition of problem and criteria for inclusion and exclusion,
(b) criteria for evaluation of studies,
(c) search strategy and
(d) data extraction (Badger et al., 2000).

While literature review helps researchers gain some background knowledge about the research topic of interest, the process may affect their preconceptions about the topic, thereby limiting their curiosity and creativity (Chang, Fung and Chien, 2013). It is therefore common to complement literature review with other foresight methods. For example, Chapter 4 describes how literature review was combined with patent analysis to conduct technology insight.

Patent analysis

Patents and patent portfolios are important assets. Companies should have appropriate structure and processes to analyze existing internal and external patents, to enable proactive management of their patent portfolio for optimization of value.

Patent analysis is the process of reviewing large volume of patents to identify certain key characteristics, patterns and trends, and interpreting the results for the purpose of technology management for the future. In general, there are two approaches for strategic technology management. The first is the bibliographic approach that uses bibliographic information such as international patent codes and citations, widely used to identify inventors and assignees. Information such as abstracts, invention descriptions, geographic protection and claims from patent text can be extracted to observe technological patterns, trends and opportunities. Analysis of the claim information data allows one to assess the technological importance of its application and the company's technical capability along similar dimension. Citation information data are useful in determining the originality and relevance of an invention and the significance of its relationships with existing and future patents. Geographic protection information gives an indication of the assignee's investment to achieve international market coverage. The second approach focuses on value creation by examining the economic and strategic value of patents using databases or survey tools to assess the impact of their technological innovation on the company value. The economic value comprises the market value and financial performance of patents, while the strategic value captures that strategic importance of patents within the company (Grimaldi et al., 2014). Chapter 4 describes the application of patent analysis, where patent data were extracted, analyzed and interpreted to provide valuable technical information used to plot the growth trajectory of technologies over time.

Text/data mining

As the volume of data captured from multiple sources continues to grow exponentially, the data including textual information form a rich repository that can be mined for use in foresight to identify new research topics and address future issues. Text mining typically involves four steps (Kayser and Blind, 2017):
(a) selecting the relevant data source for retrieval from databases (e.g. patents) or manual extraction from unstructured sources (e.g. social media),
(b) transforming the data into formats that can be read by computer programs for further processing,
(c) analyzing the data using statistical or data mining methods such as clustering and regression to determine relationships among the key variables, and
(d) applying the domain knowledge to interpret the results in the context of the foresight process.

As the text/data mining process is iterative, the results are likely to flag out new issues or stakeholders that require further search and research tasks such as focus groups or interviews to address them.

Social network analysis

Social network analysis is a method that encompasses theories and models in relational concepts or processes that are typically applied to analyze policies and their implementation (Lienert, Schnetzer and Ingold, 2013). The network boundaries can transcend across a number of levels (e.g. national, industry, organization) to enable identification of actors, analyze their relational patterns, and their structure in the planning processes. For example, in Switzerland, water resource infrastructure planning was traditionally dominated by engineers and local authorities that had relatively shorter-term objectives. When the research program introduced social network analysis to identify and invite relevant horizontal and vertical stakeholders, there was a better understanding of the complex interactions and interests of the diverse stakeholders, enabling the generation of more creative solutions at multiple levels.

Scenario stories

To be effective and creative in formulating strategies, an organization should look further into the future (long-range planning 10–50 years) beyond the usual strategic planning cycle (mid-range planning 5–10 years) while considering its vision in the context of its operating environment. Scenarios enable the organization to achieve both planning horizons, by considering a range of most likely, most challenging or most desirable possible future states (Bezold, 2010). Scenarios are essentially stories describing future events to help organizations understand in which possible ways the future can unfold. The concept of scenario planning was pioneered by Royal Dutch Shell in the 1970s to complement traditional forecasting tools, to enable the organization to respond more effectively than its competitors to the 1973 oil crisis. Since then, scenario planning has been developed and refined to be incorporated as part of strategic foresight to support strategic planning. In summary, the scenario development process involves four steps (Wulf et al., 2013; Shoemaker, 1995):

(a) Definition of scope that comprises identifying core problems and stakeholders to set clear and achievable goals
(b) Analysis of perception that captures feedback from stakeholders in at least two rounds to compare the mental models between the internal and external stakeholders about how each of the PESTEL factors can potentially impact on the organization's performance and their uncertainty so as to provide a more holistic view of the possible states of the future. Factors that are ranked significantly higher by external stakeholders than by internal stakeholders are identified as possible blind spots (areas that have been overlooked). Those factors that have been named only by a few stakeholders in the initial round but highly rated for impact and uncertainty by all in the subsequent round may be considered as

weak signals or preliminary indicators of future changes in the environment. Analysis of blind spots and weak signals will allow the organization to identify factors of influence as input to the next step of trend and uncertainty analysis

(c) Analysis of trend and uncertainty that involves the compilation and evaluation of factors to define relevant future trends through interviews with experts or computer-aided modeling for factor analysis. The relevant factors are then clustered on a grid along the dimensions of uncertainty and impact. Those factors that are rated high in uncertainty and strong in potential impact are identified as critical uncertainties, which can be used as input to the next step of scenario building

(d) Building of scenarios that is based on the two key uncertainty factors identified in the previous step of analysis of trend and uncertainty. With the projection of the extremely positive and extremely negative outlook of both factors, four scenarios are generated as four quadrants of a matrix. The influence diagrams showing the series of causes and effects that result in different events are developed to ensure consistency among the scenarios. Based on the influence diagrams, the stories or narratives of each scenario are generated. These scenarios will serve as input for defining strategic options for subsequent phases of SFM.

Chapter 5 depicts how organizations generate and use scenario stories of their possible future situations to identify capabilities for future development so as to exploit new opportunities presented in the scenarios.

Delphi survey

The validation of future scenarios constructed in strategic foresight is commonly conducted with experts using the Delphi survey. The Delphi approach has been used extensively to forecast the probability and timing of future realities by inviting the experts to provide their perspectives. Their responses are then compiled and shared with the same respondents to allow them to change their perspectives given the benefits of others' views. Through anonymity of expert participants and iteration of survey rounds with result sharing, the Delphi survey aims to converge their responses towards one forecast result to facilitate prioritization of response options that will have implications on future resource allocation. This convergent approach has been adopted across multiple disciplines ranging from public policy to technology foresight. For example, public policy makers from Japan, South Korea and Singapore have applied the Delphi approach for national foresight studies for long-range R&D planning (Cheah et al., 2019; Lee et al., 2015). The method can also be employed in various situations ranging from one with limited information to another with munificent data (Hung, Lee and Wang, 2013). For example, scholars have also used the approach for eliciting the opinions of experts to enhance the flexibility of supply chain (Lummus, Vokurka and Duclos, 2005).

Chapter 6 provides an example of how organizations can validate their future R&D roadmaps with experts using Delphi survey to rate the significance, capability level and timing of their technology and R&D forecast.

Roadmapping

The concept of roadmapping was first introduced by Motorola in the 1970s to support their strategic planning of products and technologies. According to the CEO of Motorola Bob Gavin, a roadmap is "an extended look at the future of a chosen field of inquiry composed from the collective knowledge and imagination of the brightest drivers of change in that field" (Cetindamar, Phaal and Probert, 2016). The method was initially adopted by other large technology-intensive firms in the consumer electronics, aerospace and defense sectors, before spreading out to many other areas across a wide range of industries. A key benefit of the approach is the communication associated with the development and dissemination of roadmaps, particularly for aligning technology and commercial perspectives, as well as balancing market 'pull' and technology 'push'. Communication roadmaps can take many forms, but the most general and flexible approach for developing roadmaps comprises a visual time-based, multi-layered chart, enabling the various functions and perspectives within an organization to be aligned, and providing a structured framework to address three key questions: Where do we want to go? Where are we now? And how can we get there? (Phaal and Muller, 2009). The roadmap framework can be considered as a dynamic business or systems framework, with the architecture of the roadmap providing a coherent and holistic structure within which the development and evolution of the business or system and its components can be explored, mapped and communicated.

Chapter 6 presents how an organization generates an integrated roadmap using:
(a) the market and business drivers gleaned from horizon scanning depicted in Chapter 3,
(b) the technology and R&D levels, and required resources and capabilities inferred from patent analysis and literature review in Chapter 4, and
(c) the findings on new applications with high potential impact from scenario stories in Chapter 5.

Customer discovery

The customer discovery process (Blank, 2013) seeks to understand customer needs and uses a hypothesis-driven approach to determine the value proposition of a new application. By turning hypothesis into prototype, which is also known as a minimum viable product (MVP), the process encourages putting that prototype or MVP in the hands of stakeholder or potential customer to gather feedback. Based on the feedback, the prototype or MVP can be refined with an improved version or replaced with a totally different one. The process requires iterative loops of stakeholder/customer feedback and MVP enhancement until a product-market fit can be attained with minimum product development costs.

The customer discovery process comprises four phases:
(a) Phase 1: Stating the problem statement,
(b) Phase 2: Testing the problem statement,
(c) Phase 3: Testing the value proposition, and
(d) Phase 4: Verifying the value proposition or pivoting.

Chapter 7 provides an example of how the commercialization strategy was developed with customer discovery process in the Intervention phase.

Quality function deployment

Quality function deployment (QFD) is a method developed by Yoji Akao in Japan since 1966 to help transform the voice of the customer into engineering characteristics for a product (Akao and Mazur, 2003). It is an approach that considers qualitative customer requirements and transforms them into quantitative technical specifications for product development. It involves four phases: (a) translating customer needs into product characteristics, (b) translating product characteristics into part characteristics, (c) translating component characteristics into production process and ultimately, and (d) translating production process into a plan.

One key method used in QFD is the House of Quality. It is a planning matrix that classifies customer requirements and ranks them in order of importance. Subsequently, these requirements are matched to relevant design characteristics in ranking of correlation. To build the House of Quality, it is important to first understand the needs of the customer, followed by the importance of these needs to the customer. This can be collected through engagement or experience with the customer. These requirements are then translated into design specifications and changes in each specification will affect the perception of the customer.

The House of Quality is developed by listing the customer requirements in order of importance gathered through interview sessions with various stakeholders, comprising technology and industry experts. These requirements were then translated into design characteristics with the input of the key stakeholders. It is important to note that the House of Quality is built based on the preliminary information collected and is therefore a cross-sectional analysis of demand at the point of study. As market demand changes continuously, building the House of Quality is an ongoing dynamic process that can and should be updated and enhanced as and when more up-to-date and pertinent data about customer is available. Chapter 7 illustrates how the quality function deployment framework was used in formulating an organization's commercialization strategy.

Sarah Cheah

3 Market Insight: Horizon Scanning of Service Robotics Landscape

On January 31, 2018, Edmund Ooi sat in the R&D office of the National Robotics Programme (NRP) Office in Singapore, hunched over a sizeable amount of research findings his team had gathered. Launched in 2016 by the national research agency, Agency for Science, Technology and Research (A*STAR), NRP aimed to address the country's manpower constraints in labor-intensive industries such as healthcare and cleaning through the development and deployment of robotics and automation technologies over three years. As the R&D Head, Ooi and his small but experienced team of four research officers had been entrusted with the responsibility of developing Singapore's R&D capabilities in robotics through competitive grant awards to promising robotics-related R&D projects led by public research institutes. As the financial year of 2017 would draw to its close in April 2018, the team initiated a R&D roadmapping project in the final quarter of 2017 to scan the horizon for service robotics market and technology trends, with the view to developing a roadmap in the key research areas to meet future market demand. The team had just completed several months of intensive horizon scanning of the global robotics landscape, with specific focus on the healthcare and environment domains in Singapore. As Ooi flipped through the horizon scanning report, he pondered on which aspects of the two domains should be given priority for future R&D funding. At first glance, these domains seemed to hold great opportunities for robotics development and deployment that would immensely improve productivity and push Singapore one step further towards its vision of being a Smart Nation. In healthcare, he assessed the potential of smart hospitals, staffed with autonomous robots performing a variety of tasks from cleaning and delivery to even surgical operations. In the environment domain, he envisaged fleets of modular and self-configurable robots cleaning Singapore's busy streets, alongside smart robotics systems to revolutionize garbage sorting and recycling. The possibilities for robotics applications seemed myriad. However, given that the resources on hand were limited and many capabilities had yet to be developed, the team had to decide on which aspects of healthcare and environment domains to focus on for robotics development and deployment over the next seven to ten years.

Note: The author(s) wrote this case solely to provide material for class discussion. The author(s) do not intend to illustrate either effective or ineffective handling of a managerial situation. The author(s) may have disguised certain names and other identifying information to protect confidentiality.

https://doi.org/10.1515/9783110672916-003

Singapore's service sector

Due to its smallness of size and lack of natural resources, Singapore's service sector was the largest contributor to its gross domestic product (GDP) in 2017,[1] adding S$233[2] billion in value to the economy. The service sector was projected to grow at a compound annual growth rate (CAGR) of 7.7 per cent across all variants of services including business services, transport and storage, information and communications. However, with labor shortage and rising wages in recent years, robotics and automation were increasingly seen as the primary solution to address these challenges. In 2015, the then deputy secretary-general of National Trades Union Congress, Chan Chun Sing,[3] urged companies in the service sector to utilize more technology in their operations to improve productivity. "How competitive we are as a small economy depends on how fast we innovate," he said.

One service-dominant sector in Singapore was the health services industry,[4] which contributed S$9.8 billion in value added to the economy in 2017, predominantly due to hospitals (52.8 per cent) and western-medicine clinics (23.9 per cent). Salaries and wages were the largest business cost at 49.5 per cent in the health services industry, providing an impetus for the introduction of automation and robotics. The cleaning industry, on the other hand, faced the issue of heavy reliance on low-cost and low-skilled foreign labor due to the tight domestic labor market. In 2017, 965,200 low-skilled foreign workers[5] were employed in Singapore mainly for the construction and domestic cleaning industry, making up 26.3 per cent of total employment in Singapore. To reduce foreign labor dependence, similar calls for robotic solutions were made to the companies in these industries.

---

1 Singstats, "Singapore Services Sector 2017", accessed March 20, 2019, https://www.singstat.gov. sg/~/media/Files/visualising_data/infographics/industry/singapore-services-sector-2017.pdf
2 S$ = Singapore dollar; S$1 = US$0.73 on July 1, 2018.
3 Joanna Seow, "More targeted support for automation efforts in service industry", April 6, 2015, accessed March 20, 2019, https://www.straitstimes.com/singapore/more-targeted-support-for-automation-efforts-in-service-industry.
4 Singstats, "Singapore Health Services Industry 2017", accessed March 20, 2019, https://www. singstat.gov.sg/modules/infographics/media/Files/visualising_data/infographics/industry/health-services-2017.
5 Ministry of Manpower, "Foreign Workforce Numbers", accessed March 20, 2019. https://www. mom.gov.sg/documents-and-publications/foreign-workforce-numbers.

Research, innovation, and enterprise, 2016–2020 (RIE2020)

In January 2016, Singapore Prime Minister Lee Hsien Loong (PM Lee) announced that the government would be increasing its investment in research, innovation and enterprise (RIE) for the next five years as part of the RIE2020 plan.[6] S$19 billion or 1 per cent of the country's GDP was to be set aside for the funding of science and technology research and commercialization. Speaking on the motivation for this move, PM Lee highlighted "RIE will continue to be important to secure our future" while its five-year plan from 2016 to 2020, also known as RIE2020, would make "four major shifts to capture more value from our investments and research."[7] Four major domains were chosen in accordance with Singapore's competitive advantage and their potential to contribute to national needs and achieve its vision of becoming a Smart Nation.[8] These were advanced manufacturing and engineering (AME) that was allocated S$3.2 billion at 17 per cent of the RIE2020 budget, health and biomedical sciences (HBMS) S$4 billion at 21 per cent, services and digital economy (SDE) S$0.4 billion at 2 per cent and urban solutions and sustainability (USS) S$0.9 billion at 5 per cent. Robotics was identified as a key technology to enable the four major domains of RIE2020, and NRP was established to develop the robotics ecosystem for the country. See Figure 3.1.

National robotics programme (NRP)

NRP was set up in 2016 to address the country's labor crunch issues in labor-intensive industries such as healthcare and cleaning through automation and robotics technologies. In 2016, the Singapore Finance Minister Heng Swee Keat announced that over S$450 million in funding was to be set aside to support the NRP over the next three years, citing the importance of developing technologies to drive industry-level transformation, "robotics technology can enable us to work more effectively in a tight labor market, and can also create more high value-added jobs."[9] The NRP

---

6 National Research Foundation, "RIE 2020 Plan", accessed March 20, 2019, https://www.nrf.gov.sg/rie2020.
7 Judith Tan, "S$19b R&D fund includes new value in 4 technology domains", July 22, 2017, accessed March 20, 2019, https://www.businesstimes.com.sg/government-economy/s19b-rd-fund-includes-new-value-in-4-technology-domains.
8 Smart Nation Singapore, "Transforming Singapore Through Technology", accessed March 20, 2019, https://www.smartnation.sg/.
9 Nilanjana Sengupta, "Singapore Budget 2016: More than S$450 million to support National Robotics Programme over next 3 years", March 24, 2016, accessed March 20, 2019, https://www.

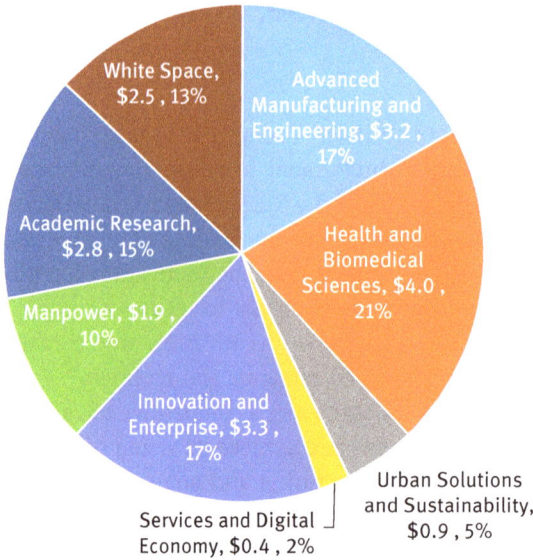

Figure 3.1: Breakdown of $19 billion RIE2020 investments (S$ billion).
Source: National Research Foundation, "RIE 2020 Plan", accessed March 20, 2019, https://www.nrf.gov.sg/rie2020

would steer the development and deployment of robotics technologies in growing service-oriented sectors like healthcare, manufacturing and logistics. It would be "the driving force behind the nationwide industry transformation maps (ITM) for robotics in Singapore."[10] As a Smart Nation, NRP would identify technologies to improve productivity, sustainability and livability, with a focus on robotic solutions to address societal challenges such as aging population, in addition to manpower crunch.

Since the establishment of the Office, NRP had been working closely with multiple public sector agencies to identify problem statements that could be addressed with the introduction of robotics technologies. The suitability of the technologies would be evaluated in three aspects: (a) ability to meet national needs, (b) ability to solve manpower shortage and (c) ability to address aging population issues. By January 2018, the team had invested in several key robotic research areas including

---

straitstimes.com/business/economy/singapore-budget-2016-more-than-450-million-to-support-national-robotics-programme.
10 ACN Newsire, "Singapore International Robo Expo 2018 returns against Exponential Change in Industry", October 4, 2018, accessed March 20, 2019, https://www.asiaone.com/business/singapore-international-robo-expo-2018-returns-against-exponential-change-industry.

end-effectors with integrated perception, autonomous vehicles and modular and self-configurable robots.

To meet the needs of the society such as urban mobility, healthcare and sustainable living, and those of enterprises for ease of doing business, the Singapore government launched in November 2014 the Smart Nation Initiative. The Initiative aimed to build a "nation where people live meaningful and fulfilled lives, enabled seamlessly by technology, offering exciting opportunities for all." This national priority was in line with the country's strategy to develop a knowledge-based innovation-driven economy that could drive its growth and global competitiveness.

Economists had identified achieving sustainable productivity as a pressing issue that Singapore had to resolve.[11] These concerns belied a slowdown in the country's workforce due largely to declining fertility rates, and the Deputy Prime Minister Tharman Shanmugaratnam cautioned that Singapore must "work on the basis that there will be no further manpower growth in the industry. The heavy reliance on low-skilled workers also cannot continue."[12] The major determinant for Singapore's economy in the long term would be productivity growth. As the size of service sector grew, the ability of the economy to boost productivity growth rate in this sector would be crucial.

Like most developed nations, Singapore faced an aging population, leading to a slowdown of workforce and labor productivity growth. Between 1965 and 2017, Singapore's population grew from 1.9 million to 5.5 million. However, the number of citizens aged 65 and above had increased rapidly, as population growth slowed down. Besides aging workforce, rising healthcare costs were thorny issues related to the aging population that the government had to tackle.

To facilitate R&D planning over the next ten years, the team launched a R&D roadmapping project in the final quarter of 2017 to scan the horizon for service robotics market and technology trends. This would enable the team to develop a robotics roadmap in the strategic research areas to meet future market demand. After several months of intensive horizon scanning of the global robotics landscape, the team put together a report comprising technology insight into the following key robotic research areas: (a) robotic end-effectors with integrated perception, (b) autonomous navigation with sensor fusion, (c) on-chip Light Detection and Ranging (LiDAR) system for autonomous robotics, (d) modular robot system for cleaning robots, and (e) tactile robot skin, conducted in the innovating countries. These countries included the United States of America, the Netherlands, the United Kingdom,

---

11 Vivien Shiao, "Productivity, inequality key issues in Singapore's competitiveness", November 17, 2017, accessed March 20, 2019, https://www.businesstimes.com.sg/government-economy/productivity-inequality-key-issues-in-singapores-competitiveness.

12 Rennie Whang, " Govt launches road map to transform food services industry", September 8, 2016, accessed March 20, 2019, https://www.straitstimes.com/business/economy/govt-launches-roadmap-to-transform-food-services-industry.

Italy, Denmark, Japan, South Korea, China and Singapore. The team also assessed future market demand, with specific focus on the healthcare and environment domains that would be of great relevance to the Singapore context.

Horizon scanning

While performing the horizon scanning activity, the team encountered several challenges, of which two stood out. The first pertained to the general nature of robotics technology categorization and fragmented literature that made identification of suitable solutions difficult. The second challenge revolved around the specific context of the Singapore environment that made it hard to apply solutions that had worked well in other countries. However, as the team addressed these challenges, they also discovered opportunities waiting to be unlocked.

Categorization of robotics technologies – fragmented literature

As the team scanned the existing literature, they pored over market reports and trade journals relating to robotics to track the trends of robotics development and deployment by diverse industries and applications. While the general categories used by these publications might be useful for understanding the prevailing adoption rate at broad industry levels, they were however too broad for searching and identifying possible applications for solving industry problems.

The broad categorization was worsened by the lack of standardization among the market analysts generating the industry publications. It was compounded by the fact that the scientific community seemed to use a different taxonomy for classifying robotics research knowledge in scientific journals and patent databases. Ooi cited the cleaning robot as an example.[13]

> But cleaning robot has many categories. We're talking about home cleaning, commercial cleaning, industrial cleaning. Home cleaning is basically just sweeping and vacuuming. But if you go to commercial cleaning there is wax scrubbing, wet vacuuming, even heavy grime kind of scrubbing technologies.

To tackle the issue of fragmented literature, the team had to delve into the topic to make further inquiry to identify the relevant stream of literature. Ooi highlighted, "if you go deeper you can mostly get what you want."

Besides cleaning, the team also conducted a search on a range of other technologies including robotic end-effectors, also known as 'grippers', which were found

---

13 Interview with Ooi, March 14, 2019.

to be classified under a basic categorization of technology called picking. However, on diving more deeply, the team found that there were myriad picking technological applications that varied widely along multiple dimensions such as the speed of the gripping process, the structure of items being gripped and the gripper's level of automation. What was crucial to this challenge was therefore the need to be specific in the search process and dive deeply into the scientific specialization of the technology applications.

To do this, the team scanned both practitioners' and academic reports, combing through the work of many companies ranging from end-effector startups to system integrators along the hallways of international exhibitions and conferences. For example, the team went to the world's largest automation exhibition, the biennial Automate Show 2017 in Chicago attended by tens of thousands of people. A wide range of companies participated as exhibitors to sell on-the-shelf advanced robotic grippers as well as offer customized end-effector solutions to customers that would require specific "pick and place" functions.

At the event, the existing pick and place end-effectors in the market were found to be specific in their tasks and the type of objectives for picking.

> For example, if … [the existing robotics companies] are working with Fast Moving Consumer Goods [customers], they will have specific pick and place end effectors for, let's say hygiene products, so they cannot make a generic hand like human's that can pick anything. They always have to pick and choose the categories of customer base that is largest for them to solve.

"A lot of people [are] selling, but not enough people developing [solutions]" was the common observation among the team. It became apparent to Ooi that the constraint of the current generation of end-effectors exacerbated by the issue of fragmented literature would present a good opportunity for solving the last mile of automation – possibly a universal gripper that could pick most types of objects.

Having a universal gripper to replace the current need to purchase multiple customized grippers for picking varied object types would be ideal, but not easy given the disparate nature of robotics knowledge. To the scientific community, the current problem with end-effector gripping was identified as slippage of objects from the robot hand's grip. To the researchers who performed R&D in this area, the R&D challenge revolved around in-hand manipulation. To date, no R&D team seemed to have successfully developed a robotic hand that could mimic a human hand, and that had the intelligence to identify the object type and adjust its grip without allowing the object to slip away or be damaged.

These technology gaps meant that there was still a shortage and market demand for the next-generation of grippers that had the intelligence of a human hand. The market for last-mile automation solution was "actually still very open to development."

Applicability of contexts

Apart from the fragmented literature, the team also encountered the challenge of searching and identifying robotics solutions suitable for Singapore. What had worked well in other cities might not work well in the ultra-dense country of Singapore with a small land area of 721.5 square kilometers. In 2018, Singapore's population density ranked third at more than 8,200 people per square kilometer in the world, after Monaco and China Macao Special Administrative Region.

The ultra-high density of the country had made it impossible to simply import robotics solutions from other cities. Recalling their scan for cleaning service robots in the literature, the team was initially excited to have found cleaning robots for hospitals. However, as they investigated the solutions further, they found overseas service robots too bulky for the narrow aisles of local hospitals.

> Hospital robotics is used overseas in hospitals but they cannot come into our wards in Singapore because ours [especially subsidized wards] are too narrow ... These are contextual environment ... but you go to US, Japan, India and the single wards of any private hospitals, any robot can just walk in.

In a typical public hospital setting in Singapore, multi-specialty clinics were interspersed with acute hospital settings. Many people responsible for different services (e.g. physicians, nurses, therapists, medical assistants) would be moving around, joined by visitors wandering about in the hospital. In contrast, the hospitals in the US or Europe would be manned by a very lean staff with much less human traffic. In hospitals serving a population with high urban density, cleaning robots would get interrupted frequently with high human traffic, and therefore could not provide adequate cleaning.

Apart from hospitals, the team also studied outdoor cleaning robots for cleaning roads and pavements. They found that every country had different cleaning requirements due to the differences in landscape, climate and road design.

> Our curbs are much higher than curbs in Europe. For example, in Spain they have almost no curb, pavement users are very different from ours. Temperature, weather, humidity, rainfall can also affect [the requirements]. If you have a lot of trees, they will [shed] a lot of leaves, flowers. If it rains, everything sticks to pavement. It is very hard to clean these up by automation. In countries that are windy and dry, the leaves can get blown away easily so it is very different problem to solve. This kind of interaction is very different.

It was evident that the space constraints in Singapore would require different types of service robots to cater to its needs. The ultra-high population density of the country would make existing robotic solutions of other countries irrelevant in its healthcare and environment domains. On the other hand, this limitation presented a rare opportunity for the country to develop the next-generation of robots to address its unique requirements.

Based on the findings, it would be expedient to invest time, talent and resources in areas that would still need improvement and meet the national needs. To overcome the constraint of space, the ability of the next-generation robots to re-configure themselves into smaller modules would give them greater flexibility to navigate in tight spaces. In a larger and more structured environment, these independent robotic modules should have the ability to re-group into larger integrated modules to cover the greater area. Re-configurable robots should be able to change their form dynamically to adapt to the different types of environments. Re-configurability would therefore be an important attribute of future robots and a critical area for robotic research investment. Re-contextualizing some of these problems would not only provide solutions for Singapore, but also other countries.

The recent years had seen the emergence of the social phenomenon of a 'reverse urban sprawl', where countries would observe intra-national migration back into the city center. In some US cities, the trend of moving back to the city was driven mainly by two groups of people – the young professionals and the old retirees – who preferred the convenience of urban living and proximity to amenities.[14]

Should the current trend of 'reverse urban sprawl' persist, in ten to twenty years, many cities in the world would face the same ultra-high population density issues like Singapore. So the team was positive that if the country could develop the capability to successfully solve the problems posed by its ultra-urban environment, it would be well positioned to help other cities solve similar problems in the future.

Horizon scanning findings

The results of horizon scanning revealed interesting trends in the world market for service robots as a whole. An Allied Market Research report on robotics technology market showed that the global robotics technology market was expected to reach US$82.7 billion by 2020.[15] Of the four types of robotics technology identified in the report, the service robot ranked as the second highest revenue generating robotics after industrial robots. The International Federation of Robotics (IFR) further classified service robots into three main categories based on their applications, namely

---

14 Lucy Wesstcott, "More Americans Moving to Cities, Reversing the Suburban Exodus", March 27, 2014 https://www.theatlantic.com/national/archive/2014/03/more-americans-moving-to-cities-reversing-the-suburban-exodus/359714/, last accessed March 28, 2019.
15 Malani, Gunjan. 2015. "Robotics Technology Market by Type (Industrial Robots, Service Robots, Mobile Robots and Others) and Application (Defense and Security, Aerospace, Automotive, Domestic and Electronics) Global Opportunity Analysis and Industry Forecast, 2013 – 2020." Allied Market Research. May. Retrieved from https://www.alliedmarketresearch.com/robotics-technology-market.

professional service robots, service robots for domestic tasks, and services robots for entertainment. Among the three types of service robots, the professional service robots were projected to grow at 20 to 25 per cent annually to reach about 397,000 units globally.[16] The fastest growing professional service robot types by units installed were expected to be the ones for (a) professional cleaning, (b) public relation robots and joy rides, (c) medical robotics and (d) logistic systems. While the Allied Market Research projected healthcare industry to have the second largest market for robotics by 2020 only after the automotive industry, industrial robots are used for automation of manufacturing processes. See Figure 3.2. The findings comprised the identification of market drivers of healthcare and environment domains, as well as the key business sectors that would address these drivers, along with critical applications within them.

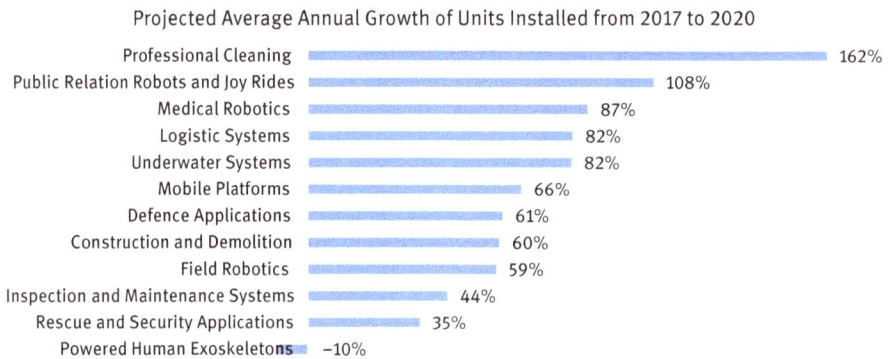

Projected Average Annual Growth of Units Installed from 2017 to 2020

Professional Cleaning	162%
Public Relation Robots and Joy Rides	108%
Medical Robotics	87%
Logistic Systems	82%
Underwater Systems	82%
Mobile Platforms	66%
Defence Applications	61%
Construction and Demolition	60%
Field Robotics	59%
Inspection and Maintenance Systems	44%
Rescue and Security Applications	35%
Powered Human Exoskeletons	−10%

Figure 3.2: Fastest growing service robots by application.
Source: Malani, Gunjan. 2015. "Robotics Technology Market by Type (Industrial Robots, Service Robots, Mobile Robots and Others) and Application (Defense and Security, Aerospace, Automotive, Domestic and Electronics) Global Opportunity Analysis and Industry Forecast, 2013 – 2020." Allied Market Research. May. Retrieved from https://www.alliedmarketresearch.com/robotics-technology-market.

Healthcare domain

Market drivers

The global healthcare industry was expected to generate around US$1.8 trillion revenue in 2017 and 2018 with a short-term annual growth rate of about five per cent.

---

16 World Robotics Report. 2017, "Executive Summary World Robotics 2017 Service Robots", Retrieved from https://ifr.org/downloads/press/Executive_Summary_WR_Service_Robots_2017_1.pdf.

The Asia-Pacific region stood as the second largest market behind North America but posted the highest annual growth rate at 11 per cent.[17] Within the healthcare industry, the medical technologies sector, which included robotics technologies, was the second highest revenue generating sector behind pharmaceutical and bio-technology, posting the second highest growth rate among all healthcare sectors (Frost & Sullivan, 2018). The medical technologies sector was expected to generate close to US$400 billion revenue in 2018, demonstrating high growth and revenue-generating potential, especially for the Asia-Pacific region.

Market analyst Gartner Inc. identified six factors that would generate greater value to the healthcare industry from medical technology.[18] Among these, three were identified as relevant to the Singapore healthcare industry according to the Healthcare 2020 Masterplan published by the Ministry of Health.[19] They were (a) emerging consumer power, (b) radical cost escalation and (c) industry structure transformation.

Having been empowered by digital technology in retail, media and personal technology sectors, consumers would therefore bring these expectations into the healthcare industry, demanding personalized experiences and automated processes.[20] Consumers' empowerment both added pressure to the healthcare industry and sur-faced gaps that could be addressed to create value through medical technologies and digitalization of healthcare services. Digitalization of clinical operations was expected to generate global financial potential of up to US$155 billion.[21]

Under the pressure of a growing and aging population as well as chronic dis-eases, the healthcare expenses for most countries had been rising rather rapidly in recent years.[22] This was no exception to Singapore, where government spending on

---

17 Frost & Sullivan, 2018, "Global Healthcare Industry Outlook, 2018: Value-based Care Will Continue to Drive Growth Opportunities for Emerging Technologies as They Move Out form Pilot Testing into Production Environments", Retrieved from https://cds-frost-com.libproxy1.nus.edu.sg/p/16399#!/ppt/c?id=K227-01-00-00-00&hq=Healthcare%20Industry%20Revenue%20by%20Sector.
18 Brad Holmes and Steven Lefeburg, "Healthcare Payer Industry Research Targets Key Priorities", February 27, 2018, Retrieved from https://www.gartner.com/document/3861476?ref=solrAll&refval=201937062&qid=386fa4411d6c480abc9feb45694499dd.
19 Ministry of Health, "State of Health: Report of the Director of Medical Services", accessed March 20, 2019, https://www.moh.gov.sg/content/dam/moh_web/Publications/Reports/2013/Report%20of%20the%20Director%20of%20Medical%20Services.pdf.
20 Cribbs, Jeff, Mark E. Gilbert, and Stephen Davies, "Healthcare Business Driver: Emerging Consumer Power" January 17, 2017, https://www.gartner.com/document/code/342010?ref=grbody&refval=3861476.
21 Singhal, Shubham, "Digital healthcare: How disruptive will it be?", May, 2017, accessed March 20, 2019, Retrieved from https://healthcare.mckinsey.com/digital-healthcare-how-disruptive-will-it-be.
22 Bishop, Mandi, and Stephen Davies, "Healthcare Business Driver: Radical Cost Escalation" January 17, 2018, accessed March 20, 2019, Retrieved from https://www.gartner.com/document/code/342012?ref=grbody&refval=3861476.

healthcare[23] increased over 300 per cent in ten years, with escalation in development expenditure over 1,300 per cent. See Figure 3.3. This was driven primarily by an aging population, who would be four times as likely to be hospitalized over a longer period and require more intensive medical care than the younger population. At the same time, a rise in chronic and infectious diseases as demonstrated by the increasing frequency of visits to primary care facilities for these diseases contributed to radical cost escalation.

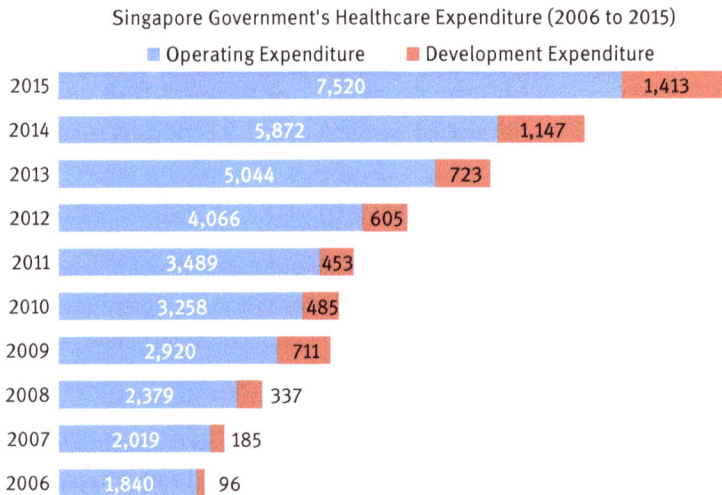

Figure 3.3: Singapore government's expenditure in healthcare.
Source: Ministry of Health, "Government Health Expenditure and Healthcare Financing", accessed March 20, 2019, https://www.moh.gov.sg/content/moh_web/home/statistics/Health_Facts_Singapore/Healthcare_Financing.html.

To manage the drivers of emerging consumer power and radical cost escalation, many countries had sought to transform the healthcare industry structure. In a similar manner, the Singapore government shifted the focus from acute care in hospitals to holistic care systems to keep patients healthy and manage chronic diseases in a long-term and sustainable manner.[24] One of the major changes in the Singapore

---

23 Ministry of Health, "Government Health Expenditure and Healthcare Financing", accessed March 20, 2019, https://www.moh.gov.sg/content/moh_web/home/statistics/Health_Facts_Singapore/Healthcare_Financing.html.
24 Ministry of Health, "State of Health: Report of the Director of Medical Services", accessed March 20, 2019, https://www.moh.gov.sg/content/dam/moh_web/Publications/Reports/2013/Report%20of%20the%20Director%20of%20Medical%20Services.pdf.

healthcare industry was the consolidation of healthcare groups announced in early 2017.[25] The structural change included integration of primary care facilities (including nursing homes, home care and day rehabilitation providers, polyclinics and private general practitioners), community hospitals and acute hospitals into three regional healthcare clusters. The integration initiative was implemented to offer seamless and more holistic care for patients at various states of health, from diagnosis and treatment to post-discharge follow-up.[26] Each cluster was supplemented with educational and research institutions to create synergy in the cluster and inject higher value creation.

Key business sectors & applications

The market drivers presented business opportunities for Singapore to explore the infrastructural designs of smart hospitals. Frost & Sullivan defined smart hospitals as hospitals that "optimize, redesign, or build new clinical processes, management systems and potentially even infrastructure, enabled by underlying digitized networking infrastructure of interconnected assets, to provide a valuable service or insight, which was not possible or available earlier".[27] Smart hospitals would focus on three aspects: (a) operational efficiency, (b) clinical excellence and (c) patient centricity. By 2025, 10 per cent of hospitals worldwide would become or have started implementations to become smart hospitals, with Canada, the Nordic regions, Australia, and the medical tourism focused regions of Singapore and Dubai being likely to lead the development in this area.

In smart hospitals, three key applications related to robotics were identified: (a) logistic management and professional indoor cleaning for operational efficiency, (b) surgical robots for clinical excellence and (c) telemedicine and rehabilitative robots for patient centricity.

Logistic management comprised the delivery, process flow, handling and packing of goods in hospitals. Automated Guided Vehicles (AGVs) could be applied to transport materials from one location to another. AGVs delivering medicine could be further integrated into an automated drug dispensing system. Performance of delivery

25 Ministry of Health, 2017. "Top 4 Conditions of Polyclinic Attendances", Retrieved from https://www.moh.gov.sg/content/moh_web/home/statistics/Health_Facts_Singapore/Top_4_Conditions_of_Polyclinic_Attendances.html.

26 Ministry of Health, "State of Health: Report of the Director of Medical Services", accessed March 20, 2019, https://www.moh.gov.sg/content/dam/moh_web/Publications/Reports/2013/Report%20of%20the%20Director%20of%20Medical%20Services.pdf.

27 Frost & Sullivan, "Future of Smart Hospitals: Concept Definition, Application, and Growth Opportunities", accessed March 20, 2019, https://cds-frost-com.libproxy1.nus.edu.sg/p/16399#!/ppt/c?id=K1FF-01-00-00-00&hq=Smart%20Hospital%20Market.

predictability had risen by 50 per cent where the per-trip cost with a robot averaging from US$5.50 for hand delivery could be reduced significantly to US$2.40 with robot delivery. Hospital data had shown that in the first year of implementation, the system could help to free up 6,123 hours that nurses previously had spent to track and retrieve medications.[28]

Professional cleaning robots for defined indoor environment could be deployed to improve operational efficiency in smart hospitals too. Between 2018 and 2020, professional cleaning robots were expected to account for about 1.5 per cent of the professional service robots installed worldwide. While their market share was not as big as logistic management robots, which would account for 48 per cent of the total professional service robots installed during the same period, professional cleaning robots show relatively high annual growth rate of 29 per cent.[29]

Advanced surgical robots could be mobilized to tackle tele-operated and robotic microsurgery. Surgical robots were expected to take up around 1.5 per cent share among all professional service robots with an annual growth of 12 per cent.[30] Several surgical robotics systems were commercially available. One of the most widely recognized systems was the da Vinci Surgical System produced by Intuitive Surgical Inc., which was already in use in some local hospitals to assist complex surgeries to improve clinical excellence of the hospitals.

Finally, assistive technologies could be applied in providing remote care to patients (telemedicine) or physical therapies (rehabilitative robots). These robotic technologies would support customer engagement and enable patient centricity in smart hospitals.

Environment domain

Market drivers

In the global market, urbanization, climate change and population growth were common market drivers for the environment domain. However, in the area of population growth, the developing economies were grappling with the issues of growing population and air pollution from industrialization. On the other hand, the developed economies faced the challenge of aging population. The key market drivers for

---

28 World Robotics Report, "Executive Summary World Robotics 2017 Service Robots", accessed March 20, 2019 https://ifr.org/downloads/press/Executive_Summary_WR_Service_Robots_2017_1.pdf.
29 World Robotics Report, "Executive Summary World Robotics 2017 Service Robots", accessed March 20, 2019 https://ifr.org/downloads/press/Executive_Summary_WR_Service_Robots_2017_1.pdf.
30 World Robotics Report, "Executive Summary World Robotics 2017 Service Robots", accessed March 20, 2019 https://ifr.org/downloads/press/Executive_Summary_WR_Service_Robots_2017_1.pdf.

the environment industry were identified as urbanization, slow workforce growth and aging population in Singapore.

With 100 per cent of its total population living in urban areas, Singapore's projected rate of change of the size of its urban population from 2015 at 5.54 million to 2020 was 1.39 per cent.[31] As the population continued to grow, it was expected to generate more waste.[32] There was an increase in total waste (including food and industrial waste) generated from 7.67 million tons in 2015 to 7.70 million tons in 2017. With intensive urbanization, there would also be greater air and water pollution, generating a greater need for professional outdoor cleaning and environment management services. However, growing demand for these services would meet with the challenge of not only a slower workforce growth, but also an aging workforce.

The labor force participation rate had grown from 67.0 per cent in 2014 to a peak of 68.3 per cent in 2015, before hovering at about 67.7 per cent in recent years, due to Singapore's policy to reduce reliance on foreign labor in selected sectors such as construction and marine sectors. From 2014 to 2016, the total workforce had grown moderately from 3.44 million to 3.57 million.

With declining birth rate, the country also faced the issue of aging population. By 2030, 20 per cent Singaporean residents would be aged 65 and above, translating into a threefold increase of aging population from about 350,000 in 2012 to 960,000 in 2030.[33] Similarly, the median age of the labor force had increased from 41 years in 2008 to 43 years in 2017.

The National Environment Agency of Singapore reported that there was a growing demand for waste recycling services in Singapore. Although there was a decrease in the amount of waste recycled due to lower amounts of wood waste, plastic and paper recycled in 2017, the recycling rate of total waste remained constant at 61 per cent from 2015 to 2017. On the other hand, there was a rise in the amount of food waste recycled at 16 per cent in 2017 by food manufacturers and wide adoption of suitable waste digesters.[34]

31 Central Intelligence Agency, The World Factbook, accessed March 31, 2019, https://www.cia.gov/library/publications/resources/the-world-factbook/index.html.

32 National Environment Agency, "Waste Statistics and Overall Recycling", accessed March 20, 2019, http://www.nea.gov.sg/energy-waste/waste-management/waste-statistics-and-overall-recycling.

33 Ministry of Health, "State of Health: Report of the Director of Medical Services", accessed March 20, 2019, https://www.moh.gov.sg/content/dam/moh_web/Publications/Reports/2013/Report%20of%20the%20Director%20of%20Medical%20Services.pdf

34 National Environment Agency, "Waste Statistics and Overall Recycling", accessed March 20, 2019, http://www.nea.gov.sg/energy-waste/waste-management/waste-statistics-and-overall-recycling.

Key business sectors & applications

The market drivers of urbanization, slow workforce growth and aging population presented opportunities for two key business sectors in Singapore's environment domain: (a) outdoor cleaning and (b) waste management. The general cleaning industry in Singapore was dominated by low value-added foreign labor, comprising a workforce of 69,000 cleaners. This pointed to a shortage of local and skilled workers in this industry, where services like predictive maintenance and asset performance management would be required.

In the waste management industry, there was a nationwide vision to improve waste collection efficiency, and robotic automation would therefore be the key to achieving this. In general, there were four phases involved in the waste management process. First, it would start with waste collection in bins that could be made into "smart waste bins" that could be fitted with sensors and some form of intelligence to collect and sort waste into various compartments by categories. Second, waste would need to be segregated by its type and suitability for recycling. Third, waste should be transported and stored at holding areas, providing opportunities for deployment of Smart Fleet Management and Logistics solutions that would involve route optimization, vehicle navigation and route planning of trucks. Finally, waste should be recycled, of which some could be recovered for further treatment and use.

The key applications in the environment domain seemed far and wide, but the team narrowed them into two areas: (a) professional outdoor cleaning and (b) waste collection and waste recycling. Professional cleaning was projected to sell 11,700 units of professional cleaning robots between 2016 and 2019. It had relatively a short payback period with low capital budgets and profit margins.[35] Projected sales of robots for domestic tasks (e.g. vacuum cleaning, lawn-mowing and window cleaning) could reach almost 30.8 million units in the 2016–2019 period, with an estimated value of US$13.2 billion. The demand for automation to undertake professional cleaning was clearly growing.

By 2030, Singapore planned to perform waste collection by smart bins which would be able to sort rubbish according to the materials. Cloud and global positioning system (GPS) technologies could be mobilized to gather data and send the nearest truck to collect waste from rubbish chutes fitted with sensors to track capacity utilization. This would improve productivity as trucks could be optimally deployed to collect from full rather than empty rubbish chutes. Smart bins could play a significant role in the future where autonomous garbage collector robots could roam the streets to collect waste.

---

[35] World Robotics Report. 2016, IFR, 2016, Retrieved from: https://ifr.org/ifr-press releases/news/world-robotics-report-2016.

In waste recycling, the waste had to be sorted into different classifications, where some categories such as food waste and metals used in electronic waste could be recycled, and proteins from wood waste could be extracted. Other categories of waste such as used batteries could be converted into low-cost energy devices, food waste into clean water and waste stream into the next-generation solid fuels.

See Figure 3.4 for a summary of horizon scanning results.

Next step

As Ooi and his team studied the horizon scanning report, he ruminated over which aspects of the two domains – healthcare and environment – should be given priority for future R&D funding. The suitability of the technologies to be funded would be evaluated in three aspects: (a) ability to meet national needs, (b) ability to solve manpower shortage and (c) ability to address aging population issues.

Both domains seemed promising for robotics development and deployment that would significantly enhance productivity and propel Singapore towards its Smart Nation vision. In healthcare, the potential of smart hospitals seemed immense, with autonomous robots performing a variety of tasks from cleaning and delivery to even surgical operations. These would not only solve the manpower shortage problem, but also address the escalating healthcare costs of aging population. However, pursuing the wide range of robotic types in healthcare would mean greater funding for diverse robotic technologies. Should the team focus on (a) logistic management and indoor professional cleaning application to achieve operational efficiency, (b) surgical robots for clinical excellence or (c) telemedicine and rehabilitative robots for patient centricity?

In the environment domain, he envisaged fleets of modular and self-configurable robots cleaning Singapore's busy streets, alongside smart robotics systems to revolutionize garbage sorting and recycling. Similar to those in the healthcare domain, these robots in the environment domain could play a significant role in addressing urbanization and sustainability issues. Although these technologies seemed to be more ready for technological adoption than those in healthcare, they could encounter more intense competition, as seen in the doubling of projected average annual growth of professional cleaning robotic units installed from 2017 to 2020 over medical robotic units. How should NRP prioritize between (a) professional outdoor cleaning robots and (b) waste collection and waste recycling robots.

The possibilities for robotics applications seemed myriad. However, given that the resources on hand were limited and many capabilities had yet to be developed, NRP had to decide on which aspects of healthcare and environment domains to focus on for robotics development and deployment over the next seven to ten years.

Market Driver - Healthcare

| Radical cost escalation | Industry structure transformation | Emerging consumer power |

Key Business Sectors

| Operational efficiency | Clinical excellence | Patient centricity |

Applications

| Logistic management | Surgical robots | Telemedicine |
| Professional cleaning (indoor) | Rehabilitative robots |

Market Driver - Environment

| Urbanization | Slow workforce growth | Aging population |

Key Business Sectors

| Cleaning | Waste management |

Applications

| Professional cleaning (outdoor) | Waste collection |
| Waste recycling |

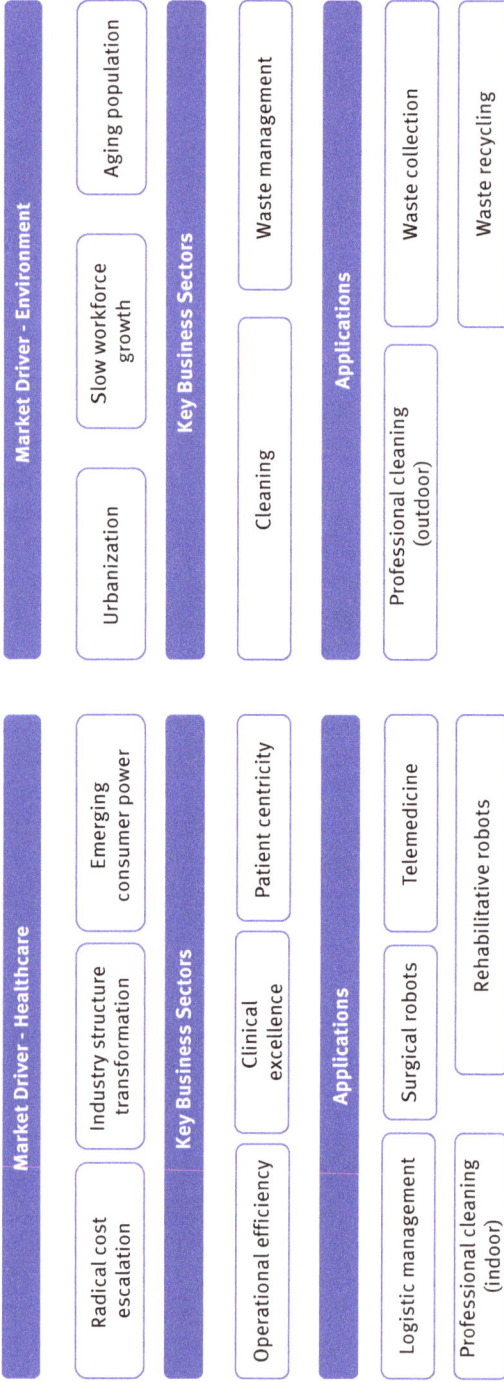

Figure 3.4: Horizon scanning summary.
Source: Author's research and analysis.

Learning objectives

This case would take the readers through the business dilemma, and present the various options available to the manager for decision-making. Through the case, the readers can appreciate the following:

- Importance of horizon scanning in intelligence gathering as the first phase of systemic foresight methodology.
- Challenges encountered in applying horizon scanning or other information retrieval and analysis processes.
- Current challenges can present future growth opportunities for organizations.
- Perspective of a national policymaker and the interplay between macro-level national considerations and market-level drivers and technological capabilities.

Sarah Cheah

4 Technology Insight: Literature Review and Patent Analysis of Service Robot Research

After spending several months on scanning the global horizon of service robotics from market reports and trade journals, the five-person R&D team at the National Robotics Programme (NRP) Office of Singapore had gathered much knowledge about the market trends. However, given the breakneck pace at which the service robotics technologies were advancing, the team headed by Edmund Ooi knew that they had to gather technology intelligence from more insightful sources such as patent databases and scientific research journals. Patent data would provide valuable technical information that could be used to plot the growth trajectory of technologies over time. Scientific research journal publications had been peer-reviewed by specialists in the relevant fields to ensure accuracy, quality, and reliability. The team proceeded to conduct patent analysis and scientific literature review for three months before using the technology insight results to support their strategic planning process of key robotic research areas for their development and deployment in Singapore's selected industries such as healthcare and cleaning over the next ten years. One of the areas that had kept Ooi's team busy in the morning of November 1, 2018, was the Modular Self-Reconfigurable Robots (MSRR) research project that was awarded a research grant by the R&D office of NRP in 2017. The project had seen the spin-off of LionsBot International Pte Ltd on February 13, 2018, that aimed to incorporate MSRR technology to provide cleaning robots as a service for commercial, industrial and public spaces in Singapore by 2019. While the team was heartened by the interest in LionsBot's cleaning robots among local cleaning companies, they wondered if the value of underlying MSRR technology could be further enhanced by the young company's organic growth or its collaboration with a strong player such as iRobot in the related technology domain. Looking at the technology insight report, Ooi hoped to use the results to guide their analysis and decision-making.

Patent analysis

Patent databases were valuable sources for tracking the evolution of technologies, as well as identifying and monitoring the research capabilities of other institutions in the market. As an important source of technical information, patent data could

Note: The author(s) wrote this case solely to provide material for class discussion. The author(s) do not intend to illustrate either effective or ineffective handling of a managerial situation. The author(s) may have disguised certain names and other identifying information to protect confidentiality.

https://doi.org/10.1515/9783110672916-004

be utilized to project the development trajectory of technologies over time. Applied at an industry level, patent analysis could synthesize useful information about the competitive strength of companies. As a fairly homogeneous measure of technical novelty over a long period of time, patents could provide detailed information at the technological class and the company level. With text mining techniques, patent analysis would enable institutions to efficiently evaluate technology sectors with low patent density to create focus for R&D activity.

To ensure generation of high-quality results, Ooi's team performed patent analysis involving four key steps. First, they took stock of their own inventory of patents in five key research areas: (a) robotic end-effectors with integrated perception, (b) autonomous vehicles with sensor fusion, (c) on-chip Light Detection and Ranging (LiDAR) system for autonomous robotics, (d) modular self-reconfigurable robot system for cleaning robots, and (e) tactile robot skin.

Second, they identified the main International Patent Classification (IPC) class. In general, patents were categorized by their classifications, the more common ones being IPC and their US Patent Classification (USPC). The team went through the initial set of patent search results to identify common keywords, which in turn helped them identify the required resources and capabilities for their R&D programs.

Third, the team visualized the patent information onto a patent map to enable analysis. In most patent databases, the patents archived would contain information such as the applicants, the inventors, the application date and the international classification number. In patent map analysis, this information was useful for creating summaries such as the patent count expressed as a cumulative patent count typically regarded as a proxy for indicating the stage of the technology life cycle.

Fourth, understanding the development stage of technology would enable the analysts to forecast future growth trajectory and predict technological limits and market maturity. Such knowledge about market saturation of the technological innovations would be useful in guiding decisions about research directions and investments. This step was critical in identifying companies with strong quantities and qualities of patents, indicating their relative technological strength in the industry. The team also went on to analyze the patent counts by country to determine the countries that were leading in certain technological innovation.

During the process of patent analysis, the team had to deal with several issues, of which two were particularly thorny: finding suitable keywords to search for relevant technologies and identifying technologies in non-English speaking countries.

Searching for relevant technologies

In the initial searches on the patent databases, the team used keywords such as "robots" or "robotics", but the search results generated were not useful. In fact, they found that patents were categorized by the basic sciences of underlying technological components. This categorization differed from the way the market analysts or business community had classified about robotics areas, and from the way the team had understood them. Ooi observed, "Patent configuration is very different from human understanding. I realized they go by product categories, number sequence, the taxonomy is very different from human understanding. It is not easy to find. It needs a lot of effort to understand."

For example, in the key research area of grippers, using such search keys as "gripper" in patent databases did not return meaningful results. Ooi realized,

> It's not easy to piece together technology at these kinds of basic levels. You need to do a lot of your own reading … to disintegrate the technology into various components and [then] understand each component that makes up the final technology.

The challenge to understand the constituent elements of a technology so that appropriate keywords could be identified and input for meaningful patent search results was exacerbated by the dearth of literature on nascent technologies. Had the team been inexperienced with the diverse scientific fields of robotics research, patent search would have been significantly daunting.

Literature review of scientific journals

To solve the problem they encountered in patent search for gripper technology, the team delved into deeper levels of the underlying technology domains. There was a scarcity of scientific research on the broad topic of "grippers", as research scientists were generally concerned with the specific components of gripper technology. For instance, gripper-related patents might pertain to the research on in-hand manipulation, which in turn might focus on a specialized aspect such as research of slippage when grippers handled various objects. Another aspect of in-hand manipulation pertained to the prediction of how to grip, where some robotic grippers would perform an analysis of the object before ascertaining the optimal mode of gripping.

Based on the literature review, the team found that the gripper technology progress could be mapped onto four levels from T1 to T4, with T1 being the most basic and T4 having the autonomous handling capability with artificial intelligence (AI). The corresponding R&D required for each of the levels were identified as R1 to R4, with R1 research focusing only on hardware design and R4 research focusing on advanced AI to perform autonomous handling, loading, unloading and transporting of materials of various sizes, shapes and forms. It was apparent that the team had to read extensively on the fundamental building blocks of the technology, immersing themselves to learn and understand the characteristics of the multiple building blocks. Ooi reminisced,

But even understanding it doesn't make it easy to search, because material properties can be used generically for almost anything in the world. For example, friction-based components [related to grippers] can be used for gripping ... for coating ... even for tires. This makes it very hard to search for patents.

The team found the need to "create a lot of linkages" between parcels of information gathered throughout the patent search process. To have a good grasp of the state of technology, the team had to study the list of patents extracted from the search, discard the irrelevant ones, annotate the relevant ones for linkages, discover new search keys from the patent contents and refine search terms before repeating the search cycle. After multiple iterations of search, they would locate a certain technology subcategory that could serve as a good lead into further patent searches.

Identifying opportunities for gripper technology

Using the search phrase: "(("robot") AND ("end-effector*" OR "end effector*" OR "grip*"))", a total of 12,808 patents were identified. The team also worked with an interdisciplinary team headed by Prof Sarah Cheah of the National University of Singapore (NUS) Business School to analyze the patent results and had several findings. First, the top assignees that had contributed to the generation of most patents were identified as (a) Intuitive Surgical Operations Inc., (b) The Boeing Company and (c) Applied Materials Inc. See Figure 4.1. The top patent holders' geographical

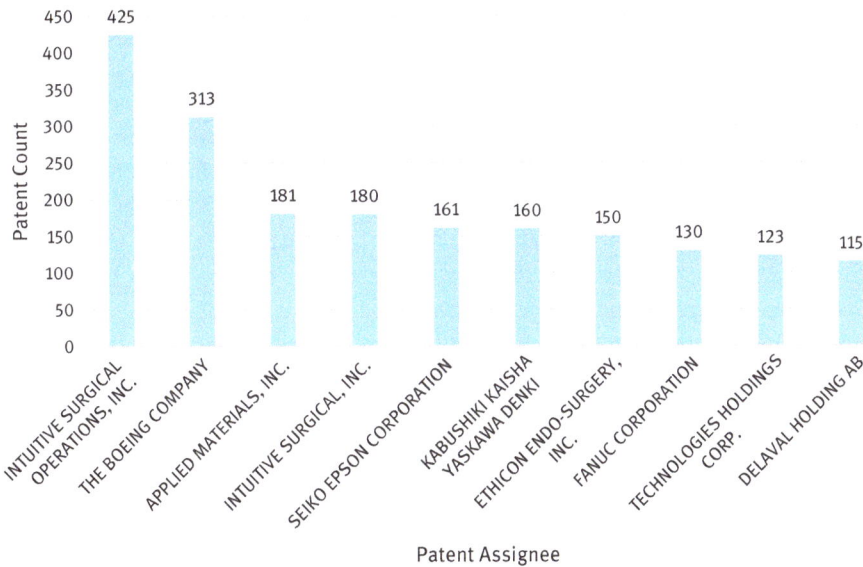

Figure 4.1: Top assignees for gripper technology.
Source: Author's research and analysis.

locations were (a) United States of America (43 per cent), (b) Europe (17 per cent) and (c) South Korea (10 per cent). See Figure 4.2.

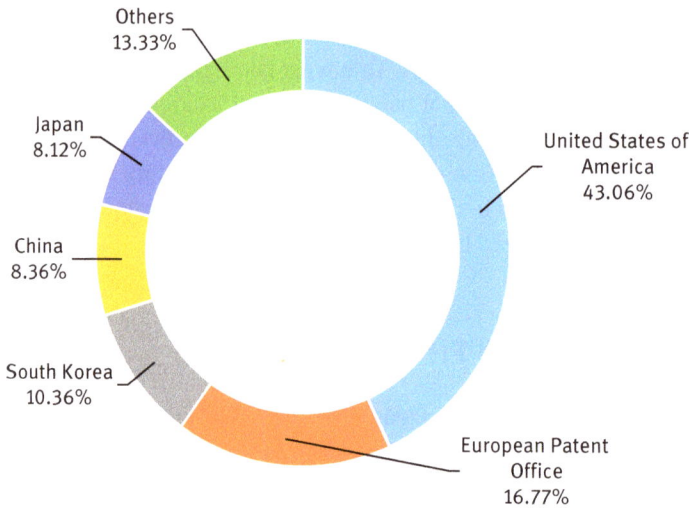

Figure 4.2: Geographical distribution of patents for gripper technology.
Source: Author's research and analysis.

Second, the majority of dominant patent holders in the robotic gripper industry developed and utilized highly-standardized robotic arms that would manipulate a specific type of object. For instance, the American company Surgical System would facilitate surgeons in complex procedures such as prostatectomies and cardiac valve repairs with standardized robotic arms. As of September 2017, 4,271 of its units had been installed worldwide, with 2,770 in the United States, 719 in Europe, 561 in Asia, and 221 in the rest of the world.[1] Each unit cost up to US$2 million and was controlled remotely by a surgeon who operates a console. The system contained four robotic arms, three of which hold surgical equipment (a scalpel, scissors and a bovie) with the last arm holding an endoscopic camera. Since there was little or no variation in the dimensions of the surgical equipment or cameras, the robotic grippers were designed primarily for maneuverability rather than intelligently ascertaining optimal modes of gripping a variety of objects. These were standardized operations which did not utilize intelligent systems to handle non-standardized objects.

It was apparent there was a lack of robotic grippers to handle non-standardized objects, presenting a good opportunity for further product or process innovation.

---

1 Intuitive, "Investor Overview", accessed March 27, 2019, http://phx.corporate-ir.net/phoenix.zhtml?c=122359&p=irol-faq.

The team surmised that it would therefore be of value to encourage the growth of companies to utilize advanced gripper technology to meet the underserved market. One such company that seized the opportunity was Hand Plus Robotics, founded by Albert Causo in July 2018.[2] The young company was a spin-off from Causo's research in Nanyang Technological University (NTU) where he was a senior research fellow, conducting research in the robotic technology subcategories of hand pose estimation, computer vision and AI. The gripper-related projects he worked on included logistics robotics for e-commerce applications and gripping systems for professional services. Out of these projects, he conceived Hand Plus that designed and built mobile picking robots for supermarkets and grasping solutions for healthcare applications.[3]

Tracking technology development in non-English speaking countries

Besides the challenge of searching for relevant technologies in patent databases, the team found it difficult to identify and track technology development in non-English speaking countries. The language barrier was a big obstacle when it came to searching for patents in such countries, particularly China, Japan and Korea. In these economic powerhouses, there existed a rich trove of patents. However, their patents were difficult to retrieve as they were filed in local languages with their countries' intellectual property office systems.

For example, when the team conducted a patent search on LiDAR technology, the search term "lidar" was input into the patent database, which yielded a total of 4,775 patents as search results. Among these, several dominant companies in the Euro-America region surfaced. These top patent assignees included Velodyne LiDAR Inc., Leddar Tech and Robert Bosch GmbH. These companies were the clear market leaders that developed innovative products in their industry. In spite of this, Ooi had a hunch that many of the non-English world's technologies were not represented in the patent search results, since the language barrier would have obscured a considerable amount of meaningful information. His intuition led him to question whether LiDAR technology had been gaining immense traction in Asia-Pacific countries whose patents did not surface in the search.

The team's hunch was validated by literature review of market reports over the Asia Pacific region. The LiDAR market in the region was forecasted to garner a

---

2 Singapore International Robo Expo, "Speakers", accessed March 27, 2019, https://www.sire.com.sg/ehome/sire2018/experthuddlespeakers/.
3 NTUitive, "Hand Plus Robotics Pte Ltd", accessed March 27, 2019, http://www.ntuitive.sg/our-start-ups/hand-plus-robotics-pte-ltd.

value of US$205.6 million by 2022, registering a strong CAGR of 25 per cent during the 2016 – 2022 period.[4] The rapid adoption had attracted growing interest in LiDAR among the governments of the countries in the region, particularly in China, Japan and South Korea, which had started using LiDAR technology in civil engineering and forestry applications. Their governments had started funneling capital and conceiving nationwide initiatives to boost the market adoption of LiDAR technology. Such developments indicated that many technological developments in the Asia-Pacific region could not be identified and tracked from patent analysis alone. It was therefore imperative to supplement the technology information gap with other channels, such as regular visits to regional trade shows.

Visiting regional trade shows and conventions for technology intelligence

In the Asia Pacific, there were certain robotics-related trade shows and technology conventions that Ooi and his team would attend, with the view to gaining insights on the ground. By speaking to the technology trade exhibitors from Japan, China and Korea, the team could gather more details about their technology progress in LiDAR applications. This direct exposure allowed the team to acquire a more holistic and accurate appraisal of the technology field, providing them information that would not have been acquired through filtering through patents in foreign languages.

Identifying resources and capabilities for LiDAR technology

Based on the patent analysis and trade show visits, the LiDAR technology progress was found to be in three levels from T1 to T3, with T1 technology on optical phased array (OPA) based on pure solid-state LiDAR with data processing system to T3 technology on application-specific LiDARs based on range and resolution cost. The corresponding R&D required for each of the levels were identified as R1 to R3, with R1 research focusing on OPA and R3 research on application-specific LiDARs focusing on range and resolution cost. The resources and capabilities required for development of the LiDAR technology comprised material science engineering, micro-electronics system engineering, data analytics, semiconductor fabrication, embedded system programming, laser/ optical physics, signal processing and conditioning and lens physics.

---

4 Allied Market Research, "Asia-Pacific Light Detection and Ranging System Market Overview", July 2016, accessed March 27, 2019, https://www.alliedmarketresearch.com/asia-pacific-lidar-market.

Assessing the commercial potential of MSRR technology

At this juncture, Ooi's team had completed the patent analysis and literature review of gripper and LiDAR technologies. In the former, the team found that there was an underserved market, and thus moved swiftly to support companies such as Hand Plus to seize the opportunity. This proved highly fruitful, with Hand Plus making plans to penetrate deeper into China's bullish e-commerce industry. In the latter, the resource and capabilities required to compete in the LiDAR market were identified for investment and development. Embarking on its final patent analysis, the team turned its attention to the MSRR technology.

Modular self-reconfiguring robotic systems or self-reconfigurable modular robots were autonomous kinematic machines with variable morphologies. In contrast to fixed-morphology robots, self-reconfiguring robots were able to deliberately change their own shape by re-arranging the connectivity of their parts to adapt to new circumstances, perform new tasks, or recover from damage. There were several classifications of MSRR robotic systems. Some of these included their structural formation, levels of reconfigurability and locomotion. See Figure 4.3 for a summary of these classifications.[5]

Using search phrases such as "Self-reconfigur", "Shape Shift", "Robot" and "Drone" for MSRR robotic systems, 1,401 relevant patents were identified. The top assignees that had contributed to the generation of most patents were Shanghai Xpartner Robotics, Shanghai Jiao Tong University, Shenyang Institute of Automation and iRobot. See Figure 4.4 for a detailed list of top patent assignees.

From the patent analysis results, the predominance of Chinese companies was clear, with the top four assignees being located within China. While this might suggest that China's MSRR market might be competitive for the entry of fledgling companies, market analysts reported the Asia-Pacific region led by China, South Korea and India was the strongest driver of future growth in the modular robotics market, projected to hold the largest market share and CAGR by 2023.[6] The buoyant market growth presented attractive opportunities for MSRR, and validated the team's earlier support of the development of this technology in August 2017 with Singapore University of Technology and Design (SUTD).

---

5 Chennareddy, S. Sankhar Reddy, Anita Agrawal, and Anupama Karuppiah. "Modular Self-Reconfigurable Robotic Systems: A Survey on Hardware Architectures." Journal of Robotics 2017 (2017): 1–19. doi:10.1155/2017/5013532.

6 Markets and Markets, "Modular Robotics Market by Robot Type, Industry, and Geography – Global Forecast 2023", October 2018, accessed March 27, 2019, https://www.marketsandmarkets.com/Market-Reports/modular-robotic-market-162980727.html.

```
Modular self-reconfigurable robots
├── Locomotion
│   ├── External
│   ├── Mobile
│   └── Coordinated
├── Structures
│   ├── Hybrid
│   ├── Truss
│   ├── Free form
│   ├── Lattice
│   └── Chain
├── Reconfiguration
│   ├── Deterministic
│   └── Stochastic
└── Form factor
    ├── Macro
    ├── Mini
    └── Micro
```

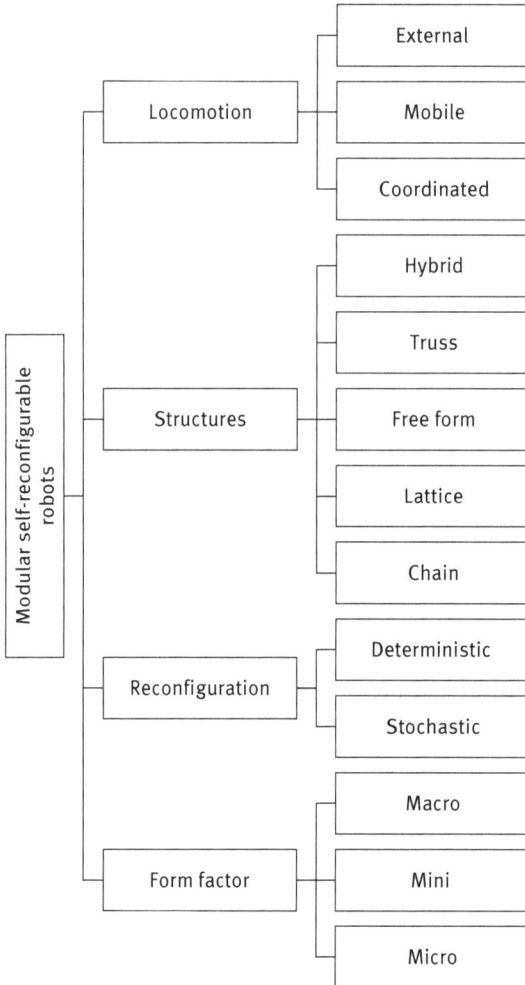

Figure 4.3: Classification of modular self-reconfigurable mobile robots.
Source: Chennareddy et al., 2017.

MSRR technology in action

Since the receipt of NRP's grant of S$4.7 million, SUTD set up a new laboratory comprising 20 researchers led by Assistant Professor Mohan Rajesh Elara to develop a series of modular self-reconfigurable cleaning robots. These robots were made of multiple square blocks that were capable of disassembling and reassembling

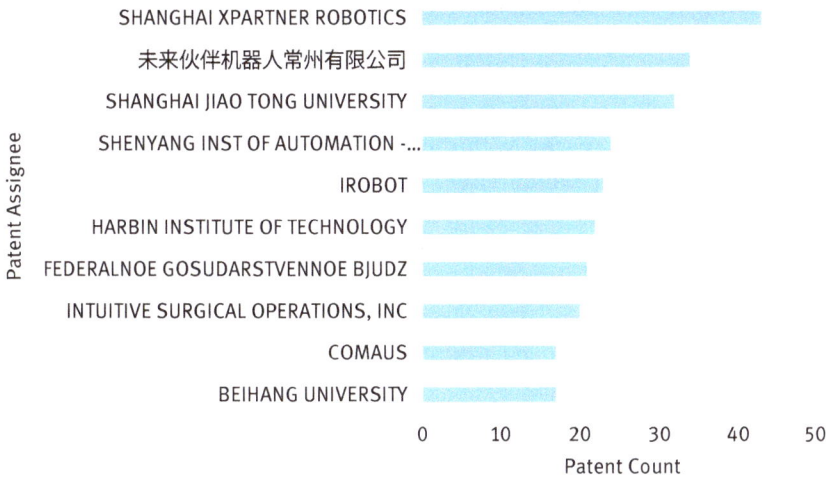

Figure 4.4: Patent analysis on modular mobile robots – top patent assignees.
Source: Author's research and analysis.

themselves into different shapes to clean different areas.[7] The design for one of the cleaning robots, hTetro named after the brick game Tetris, was equipped with infrared and bumper sensors that could clean 95 per cent of the spaces assigned to the robot. This would be a significant improvement over the current circular-shaped cleaning robot that was able to clean only 40 per cent of the area assigned. Confident that the robots would be ready for the market by 2022, SUTD hoped to license the MSRR technology to local companies to develop the robots for commercial use.

Excited by the market prospects, Mohan went on to co-found a company LionsBot with cleaning company owners Dylan Ng and Michelle Seow on 13 February 2018, and licensed the MSRR technology from SUTD to commercialize cleaning robots. Building on the MSRR research at SUTD, the LionsBot cleaning robots were more compact than the current cleaning robots available in the market, typically standing at 1.4 meters tall. At half that size, the LionsBot robots could easily maneuver indoor environments like passageways and doors. The robots did not need to be "taught" the layout and environmental characteristics of the premises before cleaning, thereby reducing their

---

7 Samantha Boh, "Shape-shifting robots may help clean hawker centres", *The Straits Times*, December 18, 2017, accessed March 25, 2019, https://www.straitstimes.com/singapore/shape-shifting-robots-may-help-clean-hawker-centres.

set-up time. Having to scan and conduct the environmental learning only once, one robot could share the computerized maps among its fleet, which used the new approach to clean intelligently in teams.[8]

The vision of LionsBot was to produce cleaning robots as a service for commercial, industrial and public spaces, with the hope to addressing Singapore's labor force crunch and aging population issue, particularly in the cleaning industry.[9] Given the initial development cost at S$1.2 million of cleaning robots over seven months, Lionsbot knew that direct sales of cleaning robots to corporate customers would not be attractive as such purchases would mean high capital expenditure and depreciation costs to them. The company continued to refine the cleaning robot concept by identifying the key cleaning tasks valued by its customers, so as to make the robots more affordable.

The first industrial model that LionsBot focused its engineering and commercialization efforts on was the fully-autonomous LeoBot Scrub robot that would perform cleaning tasks ranging from sweeping and vacuuming to carpet-cleaning and scrubbing. "The norm is to sell a [machine] costing S$55,000 to S$85,000, to a customer," Mohan observed.[10] To bring down the costs further, Lionsbot mass-manufactured these fully-autonomous robots. By careful calibration to balance between performance and price, the company was able to produce and price its robots competitively using an innovative business model dubbed as "Robots-as-a-Service" (RaaS). To encourage market adoption, LionsBot planned to launch RaaS, an offering to lease its cleaning robots to corporations, from S$1,200 per robot per month.[11] This move had captured the interest of several local cleaning companies.

After launching LeoBot Scrub robot in October 2018, the young company committed to deploy 100 units of the robot from April 2019 for rental to local cleaning companies such as Chye Thiam Maintenance Pte Ltd and Absolute Maintenance Services Pte Ltd, for their use in commercial locations such as airports, hotels and factories. Other organizations that had expressed interest were the Changi International

---

8 Asian Journeys, "LIONSBOT INTRODUCES PROFESSIONAL CLEANING ROBOTS WITH PERSONALITY", November 1, 2018, accessed March 25, 2019, https://asianjourneys.com.sg/01-Nov-2018/lionsbot-introduces-professional-cleaning-robots-with-personality.

9 LionsBot, "About Us – Robotics for better living", accessed March 25, 2019, https://www.lionsbot.com/about-us/

10 Seow Bei Yi, "Singapore firm LionsBot International to rent out cleaning robots to businesses", The Straits Times, October 31, 2018, accessed March 25, 2019, https://www.straitstimes.com/business/singapore-firm-lionsbot-international-to-rent-out-cleaning-robots-to-businesses.

11 Asian Journeys, "LIONSBOT INTRODUCES PROFESSIONAL CLEANING ROBOTS WITH PERSONALITY", November 1, 2018, accessed March 25, 2019, https://asianjourneys.com.sg/01-Nov-2018/lionsbot-introduces-professional-cleaning-robots-with-personality.

Airport and the performing arts center Esplanade. Demand had also been indicated by businesses in Australia and Japan for the cleaning robots of LionsBot, which planned to deploy 200 robots by the end of 2019.[12]

Growing organically

While LionsBot had worked hard to achieve its product development milestones, the journey towards widespread market adoption would still be a long and arduous one fraught with uncertainty and risk. With strong government support in the form of grant and infrastructure, young companies such as LionsBot were given opportunities to de-risk by developing prototypes and conducting their field trials at public places such as food centers to validate their technological feasibility and commercial viability. For example, in 2017, S$10.8 million was set aside for the National Environment Agency's Environmental Robotics Programme to develop robots to perform cleaning and waste management. With labor shortage and aging workforce, both the public and private sectors eagerly awaited automation solutions to transform the cleaning and environment industries. As the market opportunities were significant and growing not only in Singapore, but also in other cities that faced similar issues, several local companies were racing to bring fully autonomous robots to the domestic market before venturing into overseas market.

The speed at which a fledgling company had to grow its products, human resources and working capital to capture local market opportunities and adapt nimbly to compete internationally was breakneck – one that would be very challenging without strong backing from established players or deep-pocketed investors. Rather than relying on organic growth, young companies should also consider other ways to scale quickly, such as collaborating with a technology or market partner. From the findings of patent analysis and literature review, Ooi's team noticed that iRobot was the only American company in the top five patent assignees for MSRR technology, among the dominant Chinese companies. Since iRobot was a leader in the robotic cleaning industry, it could potentially add value to LionsBot and Singapore's service robotic capabilities. Possible modes of collaboration could include joint research, product development, production and marketing.

---

12 Seow Bei Yi, "Singapore firm LionsBot International to rent out cleaning robots to businesses", The Straits Times, October 31, 2018, accessed March 25, 2019, https://www.straitstimes.com/business/singapore-firm-lionsbot-international-to-rent-out-cleaning-robots-to-businesses.

A dominant player in MSRR technology

A pioneer in the robotics industry, iRobot Corporation was founded in 1990 by three members of the Massachusetts Institute of Technology's (MIT) Artificial Intelligence Lab.[13] Its Chief Executive Officer since 1997, Colin Angle, demonstrated his commitment to building practical robots that would make a difference. Explaining why the robotics industry was moving forward so slowly, he asserted that "People keep trying to make something that is cool but difficult to achieve rather than trying to find solutions to actual human problems."[14] As a pragmatic leader, he believed that "The utility of the robot needs to come first. It's [a] business model over technology."

Angle had achieved significant growth for his company, with its net worth at US$470 million in 2017 and revenue at US$1.092 billion in 2018.[15] iRobot's core competency was designing and building robots for three main functions. First, iRobot Home Robots were designed for home-cleaning purposes that included vacuuming, floor-scrubbing and pool-cleaning. More than ten million iRobot Home Robots had been sold worldwide. Next, iRobot Defense and Security robots served various military functions such as iRobot PackBot, which had performed thousands of dangerous search, reconnaissance and bomb-disposal missions in collaboration with the United States Army. Finally, iRobot Remote Presence robots provided communication solutions to emerging markets. For instance, the Food and Drug Administration (FDA)-approved RP-VITA™ telemedicine robot expanded the reach of medical care by connecting physicians with patients from anywhere in the world.[16] iRobot not only had a retail presence in North America, but also set up offices in Europe, China and Japan.

Having its own venture capital arm iRobot Ventures managed under its Corporate Development Team,[17] iRobot would engage with nascent companies that had innovative products in consumer robotics to create greater value by enabling access to its engineering and operations resources, as well as a network of external service providers, investors and partners. With a keen interest in fields adjacent to its core business including computer vision, service-based business models, robotic mobility and manipulation, iRobot Ventures would make five to ten investments per year in seed to

---

13 iRobot, "About iRobot", accessed March 25, 2019, https://irobot.com.sg/about/.

14 Dylan Love, "iRobot Cracked Open A Huge Market By Ignoring Everything People Thought About Robots", June 4, 2014, accessed March 25, 2019, https://www.businessinsider.com/colin-angle-irobot-ceo-2014-5/?IR=T.

15 iRobot, "Company information", accessed March 25, 2019, https://www.irobot.com/about-irobot/company-information.

16 Mat Smith, "FDA approves iRobot RP-VITA telepresence robot for use in hospitals", January 25, 2013, accessed on March 25, 2019, https://www.engadget.com/2013/01/25/fda-approves-irobot-rp-vita-robot/.

17 iRobot, "iRobot Ventures", accessed March 25, 2019, https://www.irobot.com/about-irobot/company-information/ventures.

Series A companies. The size of the company's investments would range from US $100,000 to US$2 million with an expected median investment size of US$200,000. iRobot Ventures' first official collaborator was a computerized 3D-mapping company Paracosm with a seed funding deal that was closed in 2014.[18] "There's a lot going on in the robotics space and really the best way to understand it is to participate in it.," said Angle in 2014. "By establishing the venture fund we're able to go out and get to know emerging companies that are building robots and robot-related technologies and get involved in these companies."

iRobot's collaboration with Paracosm allowed the young California-based startup to build its team of experts and develop better algorithms for robotics, gaming and other emerging applications that would utilize 3D-mapping technology. The collaboration was timed fittingly with Paracosm's product development stage. Its CEO Amir Rubin was optimistic for what this collaboration would enable, "It unlocks totally new applications and possibilities that have never been achievable before."[19] Looking forward, Rubin conjectured that they might commercialize one or two of the technologies they developed with iRobot.

Collaborating with an established player

Taking a leaf from Paracosm, young startups such as LionsBot could consider collaborating with established players such as iRobot Ventures to leverage their expertise, network and resources. Having access to the partner's engineering and production resources would reduce the time required to hire skilled human resources and source for qualified suppliers and procure suitable materials for product development and manufacturing. Tapping on its network of suppliers, channel partners and distributors would help move the goods and services quickly from production and distribution to target customers.

On the other hand, such collaborations would entail some costs and risks for the young startup. In exchange for access to the collaborator's capital and resources, the startup would most likely be expected to cede some equity stake and control. This could inadvertently set up the possibility of a future hostile takeover or complications in managerial matters should the company become highly profitable in the future. Arrangements regarding the ownership of IP might not be in favor of young companies, whose relatively lower bargaining power might serve as a disadvantage.

---

18 Jonathan Shieber, "The Dawn Of Our Robot Overlords Inches Closer As iRobot Starts VC Shop", January 23, 2015, accessed March 25, 2019, https://techcrunch.com/2015/01/23/the-dawn-of-our-robot-overlords-inches-closer-as-irobot-starts-vc-shop/.
19 Ingrid Lunden, "Paracosm Raises $3.3M From Atlas, iRobot To Turn Our World Into A 3D Holodeck", March 11, 2014, accessed March 25, 2019, https://techcrunch.com/2014/11/03/paracosm-raises-3-3m-from-atlas-irobot-to-turn-our-world-into-a-3d-holodeck/.

Next steps

Moving forward, Ooi's team wondered if the value of the underlying MSRR technology could be fully captured by LionBot's organic growth. Or would its collaboration with a strong player such as iRobot in the related technology domain enable the young company to create more value and sharpen its competitive advantage in the domestic and foreign markets? Looking at the technology insight report, Ooi hoped to use the results to guide their analysis and decision-making.

Learning objectives

This case seeks to highlight the following:
- Importance of the intelligence phase of SFM to define an organization's scope in foresight study.
- Introduction of literature review and patent analysis methods in the intelligence phase to identify the key technologies that are critical to organizational success.
- Illustration of how organizations face challenges in conducting technology insight and adopt responses to address them.
- An understanding of how an organization's future developments and activities can be hugely and effectively shaped by the quality of technology insight, which sets the tone for the journey forward.
- Insight into the importance of R&D collaboration between private firms and public research institutes to enable the firms' development of innovative capabilities that are critical for their competitive advantage.

Sarah Cheah

5 Assessing Future Impact: Developing Scenario Stories

On February 5, 2018, the R&D team headed by Edmund Ooi at the National Robotics Programme Office (NRP) convened to review the outcome of a series of workshops they had conducted with the scientific and business community in the final quarter of 2017. These inter-disciplinary workshops aimed to encourage participation from diverse industries to articulate their perception of possible futures with robotics in society, communicate their visions of tomorrow as a form of storytelling and develop them into narrative scenarios. The scenario stories served to promote awareness of future societal trends and disseminate knowledge about robotic technologies and their socio-economic impact, with the view to increasing social acceptance of future robotics deployment across the industries.

The events saw a good turnout of technology and industry experts at the forefront of the robotics fields, and had yielded illuminating scenario stories for inspiring future research and development directions. Ooi's team had scoped the discussion around soft robotic applications on two fronts: the broad healthcare domain, and the narrower domain of inspection and maintenance works in constrained environments. From the workshop sessions, several narratives had emerged. In the healthcare domain, scenario stories revolved around assistive and surgical devices, as well as wearables for possible deployment in the near future. Images of shape-morphing prosthetics and self-healing soft manipulators were conjured up for the distant future. The mental pictures articulated by the participants for the industrial inspection domain dwelled on flexible structures like snake robots that could conduct inspection in highly complex mechanical systems. Themes were postulated on soft structures like squishy robots that could navigate through infrastructural systems involving pipes and ducting for their inspection and maintenance.

Drawing upon these scenario stories as inspiration, the team planned to develop future robotics R&D and commercialization roadmap for various industries. To proceed, the team contemplated two possible approaches. They could either adopt the grant-call approach or the bottom-up proposal method. The grant-call approach would solicit proposals from a wide community of research performers through the mechanism of a grant call or invitation to apply for a grant from NRP. This approach would give the team the opportunity to evaluate and select the most suitable proposals from hopefully a wide pool of candidates, but at the risk of receiving proposals with competing technologies or research duplication. The bottom-up proposal method would

Note: The author(s) wrote this case solely to provide material for class discussion. The author(s) do not intend to illustrate either effective or ineffective handling of a managerial situation. The author(s) may have disguised certain names and other identifying information to protect confidentiality.

https://doi.org/10.1515/9783110672916-005

identify and invite the most suitable researchers to form a research team that would then collectively develop a proposal that would be holistic and integrated to solve specific problems. Mulling over the two approaches, the team had to decide which would be the most appropriate path to take.

Scenario planning and roadmapping

In strategic planning, an organization would generally use situational analysis tools such as Porter's Five Forces (arising from existing rivals, suppliers, new entrants, customers and substitutes) or SWOT (analyzing its internal strengths and weaknesses with regard to its resources and capabilities in juxtaposition to the opportunities and threats that it was likely to encounter in the external environment). However, in a world that had become increasingly more interconnected, the organization would face a greater level of uncertainty, exacerbated by the growing complexity and volatility of industries. Since future trends would be harder to forecast than those in the past, the organization would need more sophisticated tools such as scenario planning that would incorporate the element of uncertainty in its strategic planning, particularly in the R&D and commercialization roadmap that would span over a long time horizon of ten years or more.

Scenario planning would involve the identification of possible future states or scenarios and development plans, with the view to not only anticipating the future, but also understanding the routes to different scenarios. Scenario planning was therefore distinct from other planning techniques such as sensitivity analysis and contingency planning. While sensitivity analysis would analyze the impact of a single variable while holding others constant, scenario planning would explore the impact of multiple variables without keeping any constant so as to understand the dynamics of their interactions. For example, in the healthcare industry, multiple variables including aging population and increasing consumer expectation would be expected to contribute to a likely future state of escalating healthcare costs. Unlike contingency planning that would deal with one uncertainty such as the development of artificial intelligence (AI), scenario planning would examine the impact of multiple uncertainties such as the concurrent emergence of AI, wearable electronics and computer vision. In addition, scenario planning would involve external and internal stakeholders to capture different perspectives. The diverse views would enable the strategic planners and decision makers of the organization to identify blind spots and broaden their horizon. Compared to other planning tools, the future scenarios and their development paths would be useful for them to generate more comprehensive strategies in the form of R&D and commercialization roadmap in response to uncertainty, thereby enabling the organization to manage complexity and volatility more effectively.

In the final quarter of 2017, the R&D team of NRP organized a series of scenario development workshops with the technology and industry experts to envisage possible future scenarios of service-oriented robots at home and in the workplace. By capturing the articulation of these likely future states, the organization aimed to identify potential and emergent applications of robotics technology, that could shape the development paths to the different scenarios. These workshops had several objectives. First, they encouraged meaningful interaction and discussion among experts across multiple disciplines in the robotics community to identify future needs or problems in the society that robotics would be well positioned to address. Second, they surfaced existing gaps in robotics research and applications, suggesting opportunities for development and commercialization over the next five to ten years. Third, they identified resources and capabilities that the organization had to prioritize for investment as part of their development and commercialization roadmap. To achieve these objectives, the workshops were conducted in three stages: (a) defining the relevant domain scope, (b) understanding perception of stakeholders, impact and uncertainty, and (c) developing scenario stories. These three stages would be elaborated in the following sections with the example of a scenario workshop that focused on soft robotics.

Defining the relevant domain scope

Soft robotics was a specialized field of robotics that studied the design and development of robots that were made from soft and elastic materials for applications that were not viable with conventional rigid robots.[1] The field would involve multiple scientific disciplines ranging from material sciences and intelligent systems to mechanical and biomedical engineering. In one of the scenario workshops, the NRP R&D team focused on soft robotics. The soft robotics workshop began in broad strokes by first recapitulating the organization's vision through a quote from the Chairman of the R&D Robotics Task Force, Professor Quek Tong Boon, "We envision a vibrant and innovative robotics ecosystem capable of providing solutions to fuel the Smart Nation initiative and to establish Singapore as a global center of excellence for the study, research, development, making and application of robotics solutions." To develop a winning robotics ecosystem, the R&D team embarked on three strategic thrusts: (a) identify and develop differentiating technology research capabilities (e.g. end-effectors with integrated perception), (b) accelerate lead demand-driven robotics solutions development (e.g. healthcare and environment), and (c) enable mass adoption (e.g. government agencies, multi-national companies

---

1 Nature, "Soft Robotics", May 25, 2018, Nature Reviews Materials, accessed April 14, 2019, https://www.nature.com/collections/wpsbvwhdyh.

as well as small and medium enterprises). The workshop drew the participants' attention to two salient national imperatives frequently highlighted by the Singapore government. First, Singapore was in the process of tightening its inflow of foreign labor, tapering strongly from 80,000 foreign workers in 2011 to 26,000 in 2014.[2] Next, Singapore had been at the forefront of the Asian "Silver Tsunami", a demographic phenomenon that saw burgeoning populations of elderly. The United Nations Department of Economic and Social Affairs (Population Division) had projected a tripling of the elderly population (60 years old and above) from 719,000 at 15 per cent of the total population in 2009 to 2.067 million at 40 per cent in 2050.[3] Drawing on these imperatives, two domains were identified to frame further discussion: (a) healthcare and (b) inspection and maintenance works in constrained environments. See Figure 5.1.

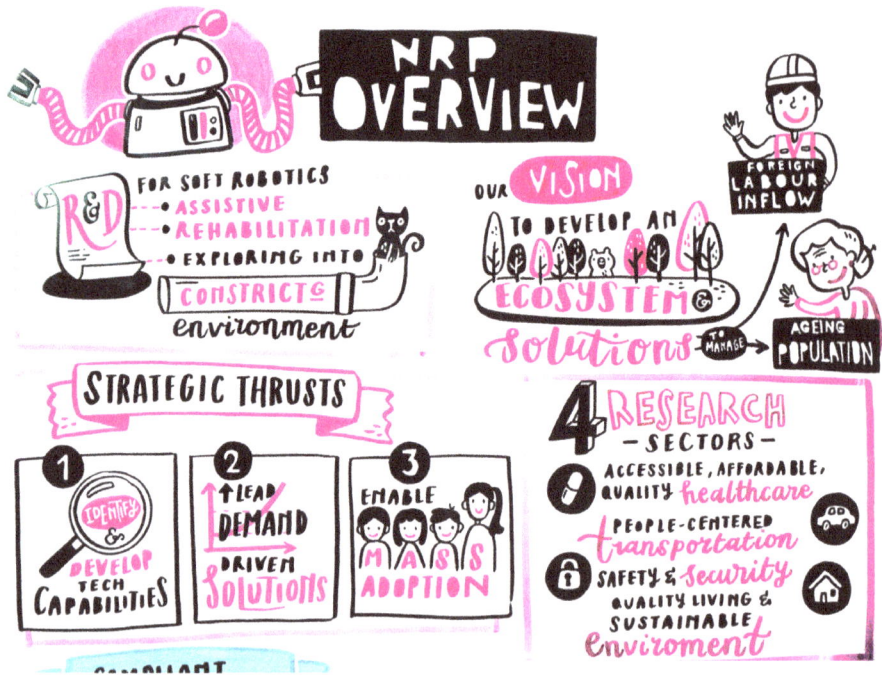

Figure 5.1: Overview of strategic thrusts.
Source: Organization document.

2 Ng Jing Ying, "Labour market will tighten further, warns Chuan-Jin," March 10, 2015, *Today Singapore*, accessed April 14, 2019, https://www.todayonline.com/singapore/labour-market-will-tighten-further-warns-chuan-jin.
3 United Nations Department of Economic and Social Affairs, "World Population Ageing 2009," United Nations, accessed April 14, 2017, https://www.un.org/en/development/desa/population/publications/ageing/ageing-development.asp.

Healthcare

Among several domains including transportation, safety and environment, healthcare emerged as one of the highest priority. The public sector was expected to lead the demand for robotics applications to enhance the accessibility, affordability, and quality of healthcare for Singaporeans. Accounting for the significance of the healthcare domain, the workshop cited its potential to generate productivity gains for Singapore, alongside its ability to support an aging workforce and improve health and clinical outcomes since the growing elderly population would drive demand for healthcare services. The workshop also identified a range of upcoming healthcare facilities including three community hospitals, four medical centers and nine nursing homes scattered across the country. Collaborative platforms existed between healthcare service providers and robotics research institutions to ensure that the solutions developed for the lead demand institutions could be eventually be adapted for mass deployment across the healthcare industry. For example, the Centre for Healthcare Assistive Robotics Technology (CHART) at Changi General Hospital was set up as a healthcare robotics collaboration platform to enable healthcare professionals to work closely with academia, industry and research institutions to develop impactful healthcare solutions leveraging on robotics and assistive technology.[4] It aimed to focus on four key areas including automating manual work, enhancing rehabilitative technology, developing robotics-enabled "smart wards", and designing assistive technology for the aged with the goal of mass market adoption throughout the Singapore healthcare industry.

Out of CHART was a grant jointly organized by the Ministry of Health's (MOH) Smart Systems Programme Office (SSPO) and the NRP in 2018, known as the Singapore Health Assistive and Robotics Programme (SHARP) Grant.[5] By 2020, it was projected that there would be more than 12,000 acute and community hospital beds in Singapore. A rapidly aging population accompanied by a rise in chronic disease would mean higher demand for healthcare services. To meet the growing needs, the SHARP Grant aimed to catalyze research and innovations of assistive and robotics technologies for medical services. The SHARP Grant identified three distinct priorities to tackle through funding the appropriate technology developments: First, it sought to enable productivity gains by reducing heavy reliance on manpower. For example, grant applicants were expected to achieve the reduction of staff-to-patient ratios in hospitals for the next five years, starting with nurses and ancillary staff, thereby enhancing productivity by 20 per cent. Next, it aimed to

---

4 Changi General Hospital, "CGH Launches Healthcare Robotics Centre to Drive New Solutions in Healthcare", July 23, 2015, accessed April 5, 2019, https://www.cgh.com.sg/newsroom/Documents/ 2015/23%20Jul%20-%20CGH%20Launches%20Healthcare%20Robotics%20Centre%20to%20Drive% 20New%20Solutions%20in%20Healthcare.pdf.
5 National Health Innovation Centre, "Singapore Health Assistive and Robotics Programme Grant", accessed April 5, 2019, http://nhic.sg/web/index.php/sharp-programme.

support Singapore's aging population and workforce by applying robotics in developing "hospital to homes" delivery systems, promoting healthy living and motivating functional independence. Finally, it strove to improve health and clinical outcomes by extending human capabilities and functionalities. With two focus areas – "Hospitals of the Future" and "Hospital to Home", NRP had secured funding led by the Ministry of Health, to develop healthcare robotics and assistive program to solve national imperatives. The first focus area described the desire to build "smart healthcare institutions" embedded with robotics-enabled precision care, with the goal of delivering higher quality services with less manpower. The second was concerned with robotics-enabled care within the home environment, enabling elderly Singaporeans to age longer and better at home to reduce their reliance on full-time caregivers.

Inspection and maintenance works in constrained environments

Land scarcity in Singapore was a perennial challenge to the country's urban development since its early independence in 1965. The Urban Redevelopment Authority was established in April 1974 to oversee urban design, land-use planning and development control – functions that were critical to address the country's land shortage issue and its impetus for efficient and optimal land usage. As part of an initiative introduced in 2005 to drive Singapore's construction industry towards more environment-friendly buildings, certified "Green Mark Buildings" were becoming prevalent as existing buildings were converted while new buildings were developed to meet the certification standards. A 2013 report by the Building and Construction Authority (BCA) in Singapore forecasted that by 2030, Singapore would have had 80 per cent of its buildings certified with its Green Mark.[6] This would mean achieving energy- and water-efficiency with a high quality and healthy indoor environment, integrated with green spaces and constructed from eco-friendly materials. The country was on its way to achieving this goal, demonstrating its competence in a report by consulting firm Solidance that rated Singapore in 2010 as the first in Asia for its green building policy. In early 2013, research by McGraw Hill Construction also found that out of 62 countries worldwide, Singapore was most heavily involved in the development of green buildings. As at September 2013, Singapore had more than 1,650 Green Mark certified building projects totaling some 49 million square meters and accounting for 21 percent of total existing building floor space.

Owing to the country's strong desire for advanced urban development solutions, there was an increasing need to conduct inspection and interventions with

---

6 Building Construction Authority, "Leading the Way for Green Buildings in the Tropics", accessed April 5, 2019, https://www.bca.gov.sg/greenmark/others/sg_green_buildings_tropics.pdf.

more complex integrated engineering designs for both infrastructure systems and mechanical systems in the country's urban landscape. In 2017, the BCA introduced a new framework to ensure buildings were easy and safe to maintain.[7] Under this framework, it tightened the facade-maintenance regime to ensure regular and proper inspection. BCA's outgoing chief executive officer Dr John Keung stressed that Singapore's endeavor of building maintenance was concerned with both safety and productivity issues. Building maintenance "[currently] takes up a lot of manpower," he said, therefore stressing the need for innovative technologies to augment the increasing demand for urban maintenance and inspection services. "We cannot run away from a very tight labor market. So the way forward is to use as much technology as possible to help us do all these work instead of adding more workers." Furthermore, a government decision in 2018 by the Second Minister for National Development Desmond Lee mandated that building owners hire qualified personnel to conduct a facade inspection every seven years, as part of its plans to "future-proof" Singapore's existing infrastructure.[8] "As our city ages, we will need to find ways to future-proof our infrastructure so that it continues to be safe and functional," Mr Lee highlighted in the Parliament. To support inspection and maintenance works in the constrained environments of Singapore, NRP had set its sights on augmenting processes and functions in the domain with robotics technology in the hope of offsetting the manpower costs and reliance required.

See Figure 5.2 for an overview of possible robotics applications for healthcare and industrial inspection domains introduced at the first stage of the workshop.

Understanding perception of stakeholders, impact and uncertainty

At the second stage, the workshop encouraged external stakeholders to articulate their mental models of possible futures with soft robotics in the healthcare and industrial inspection domains. Using short poster sessions dubbed as the "Lightning Talk", technology and industry experts were invited to share how their current research and development work on soft robotics would shape and impact the

---

7 Rachel Phua, " BCA to introduce building maintenance framework, tighten facade maintenance regime Read more at https://www.channelnewsasia.com/news/singapore/bca-to-introduce-building-maintenance-framework-tighten-facade-8890356", May 28, 2017, accessed April 5, 2019, https://www.channelnewsasia.com/news/singapore/bca-to-introduce-building-maintenance-framework-tighten-facade-8890356.

8 Louisa Tang, " Building facade inspection to be made mandatory as city ages", March 6, 2018, accessed April 5, 2019, https://www.todayonline.com/singapore/building-facade-inspection-be-made-mandatory-city-ages.

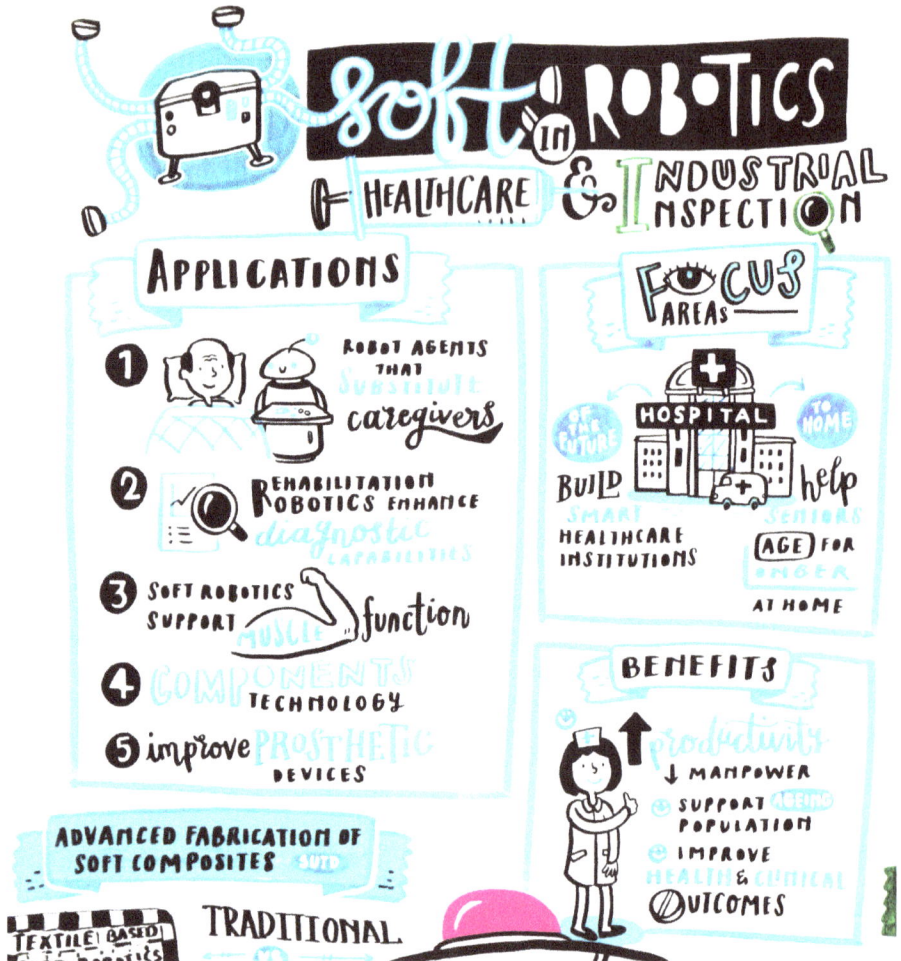

Figure 5.2: Visual summary of use cases from workshop.
Source: Organization document.

development paths to these models. They came from public research institutes such as the Singapore Institute of Manufacturing Technology (SIMTech) and Institute of High Performance Computing (IHPC), as well as university research centers including the National University of Singapore (NUS), Nanyang Technological University (NTU) and Singapore University of Technology and Design (SUTD). Nine experts shared on several aspects of soft robotics.

The first aspect pertained to physics-based design that involved mechanical engineering, robotics and bio-inspired design. For example, a scientist from NTU shared his work on robotic rehabilitation using a clutchable handle with only one motor that would offer multiple degrees of freedom to achieve 50 per cent reduction in the patient's muscle effort. A mechanical engineering research faculty from NUS introduced his work on dielectric actuators. An actuator could be defined as a device that would convert energy, typically electrical energy, into physical motion.[9] The stretchable actuators could be designed and developed to mimic human bicep and tricep muscles to mirror medical rehabilitation functions performed typically by nurses and doctors.

The second aspect was related to the use of advanced fabrication techniques such as the construction of flexible structures, multi-material 3D printing and multi-medium 3D fabrication. A research team from SUTD had integrated the technique of direct ink writing (DIW) of polymeric inks into matric materials and the 3D printing process of fused deposition modeling (FDM). By combining these two additive manufacturing processes of DIW and FDM, the team could fabricate soft robot bodies as functionalized soft composite structures.

The third aspect focused on advanced functional materials such as smart materials, elastomers and composites. A few researchers from NTU, NUS, IHPC and SIMTech articulated their application of compliant mechanisms that would use flexible monolithic structures and their elastic body deformation to transmit force from one port to another, to create artificial muscles and wearable mobility for the elderly people. These flexible structures could also be developed into soft moving robots navigating through complex or challenging environments. In particular, a biomedical engineering professor presented his work on soft wearables for different body parts including soft robotic gloves for hands, socks for feet, as well as braces for wrists, elbows and knees for rehabilitation and assistive applications in a healthcare context. The devices could also be adapted for industrial inspection and maintenance. See Figure 5.3 for an overview of the experts' perceptions of the future that influenced their research work.

The uncertainty of soft robotics might be assessed by the maturity of the soft robot industry and the technology readiness level (TRL)[10] of the underlying technologies. The industry was still considered nascent where the soft robotics ecosystem had a dearth of complementary software applications and compatible hardware components, exacerbated by a lack of standards and talent. Some soft robotics companies had failed, with the first soft robot gripper company Empire Robotics ceasing

---

9 Robotshop, "How to Make a Robot – Lesson 3: Making Sense of Actuators", September 17, 2018, accessed April 5, 2019, https://www.robotshop.com/community/tutorials/show/how-to-make-a-robot-lesson-3-making-sense-of-actuators.

10 TRL is a system developed by the North American Space Agency (NASA) to measure the maturity level of a particular technology on a scale of 1 to 9, with TRL 1 being the lowest and TRL 9 the highest.

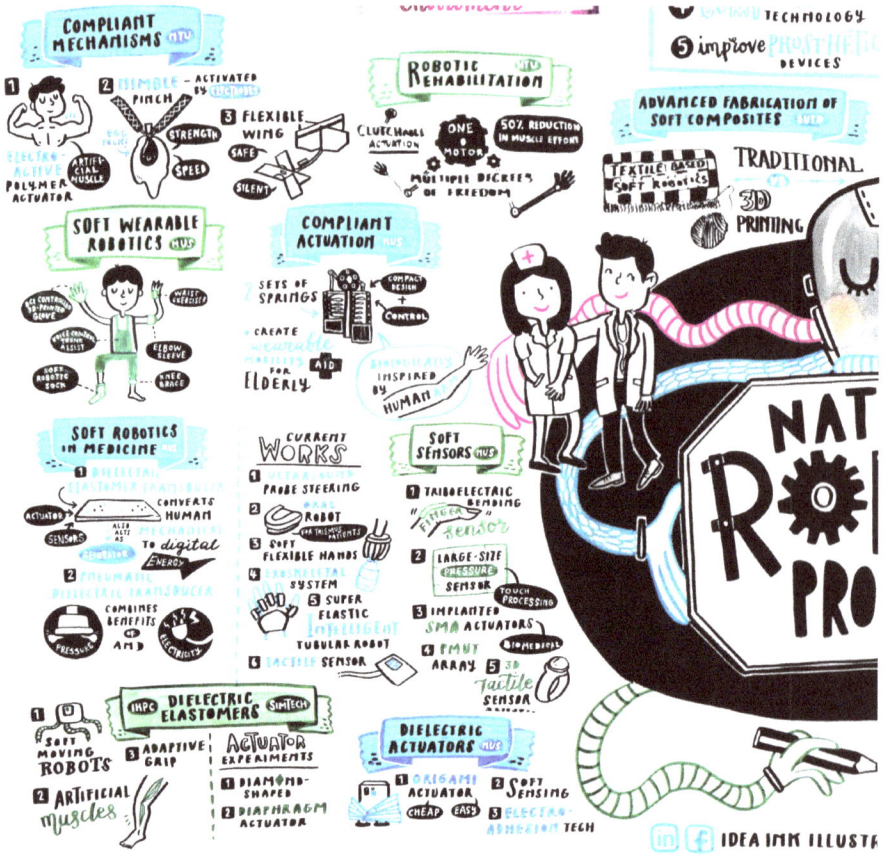

Figure 5.3: Overview of experts' perceptions of the future that influenced their research work.
Source: Organization document.

operations in 2016.[11] Rather than procuring individual grippers, customers would expect complete solutions including computer vision and machine learning to be integrated with the grippers – a demand that standalone gripper companies would not be able to meet.

A recent study was conducted on five soft actuator types that were considered instrumental in future robotics design: (a) shape memory alloys (SMA), (b) fluidic elastomer actuators (FEA), (c) dielectric electro-activated polymers (DEAP), (d) magnetic/electro-magnetic actuators (E/MA) and (e) shape-morphing polymers (SMP).

---

11 Jeremy Wagstaff, "Snake on a plane! Don't panic, it's probably just a (soft) robot", June 19, 2017, accessed April 5, 2019, https://www.reuters.com/article/us-tech-robots/snake-on-a-plane-dont-panic-its-probably-just-a-robot-idUSKBN19A0UV.

The results indicated E/MA as having the lowest TRL as it was still under development in controlled laboratory environments. SMP and DEAP were found to be moderate in TRL as there were very limited examples outside the laboratory and much development would still be required to improve the material characteristics, electromechanical design and control. SMA and FEA were the highest in TRL compared to the other soft actuator types, but they still had limited commercial work range that inhibited their commercialization into full products.[12] While the socio-economic impact of soft actuators could range from healthcare to industrial applications, certain combinations of criteria would be most important for the two target domains. In the healthcare domain, impact was found to be the greatest for soft actuators that had compliance, controllability, operation range, scalability and topology. As for industrial inspection and maintenance domain, soft actuators with compliance, energy efficiency, operation range and TRL were critical criteria for their optimal impact.[13]

Developing scenario stories

Healthcare

Building on the earlier input of stakeholders' perception from experts' presentation as well as the uncertainty and impact of the soft robotics research development, the workshop led the participants' discussion into development of future scenarios in the form of storytelling.

Three key scenarios were identified in the healthcare domain. The first was the enhancement of orthotic and prosthetic functionalities. To distinguish the two,[14] orthotics involved precision and creativity in the design and fabrication of external braces, called orthoses, as part of a patient's treatment process. Prosthetics pertained to the use of artificial limbs, called prostheses, to enhance the function and lifestyle of persons with limb loss. Soft robotics would augment the functions of orthoses and prostheses in order to mirror more closely the functions of their equivalent biological limbs. Actuators would be heavily integrated into a prosthetic limb that would require precise stretching and contractions. One example was the Skywalker Hand developed by the Georgia Technological College of Design in the

---

12 Boyraz, Pinar, Gundula Runge, and Annika Raatz. "An Overview of Novel Actuators for Soft Robotics." In *Actuators*, vol. 7, no. 3, p. 48. Multidisciplinary Digital Publishing Institute, 2018.
13 Boyraz, Pinar, Gundula Runge, and Annika Raatz. "An Overview of Novel Actuators for Soft Robotics." In *Actuators*, vol. 7, no. 3, p. 48. Multidisciplinary Digital Publishing Institute, 2018.
14 Georgia Tech, "What is Prosthetics and Orthotics?", accessed April 5, 2019, https://mspo.gatech.edu/prosthetics-orthotics/.

United States that allowed its wearer the acute ability to control each individual finger and conduct complex tasks like playing the piano.[15]

The second scenario story was soft exoskeleton gloves for rehabilitation of muscular control, frequently used in physical therapy treatment following a stroke. An example of this was the soft robotic EsoGlove developed by a Singapore-based startup Roceso Technologies.[16] EsoGlove was a Food and Drug Administration (FDA)-registered hand rehabilitation system that allowed users to "regain self-reliance in the most natural and efficient way". It comprised a Brain Computer Interface (BCI) that used non-invasive electrodes to pick up commands from the user's brain to assist the re-familiarization with various basic hand movements.[17]

The final scenario story concerned robotic agents that would substitute caregivers in patient maneuvering and activities in daily routines. Such soft robotic technologies would leverage a system of soft sensors and dielectric elastomer materials to perform tasks such as picking up and moving fragile objects (e.g. plates, glasses and eggs) that a patient might not be able to do independently. These robotic agents would assist in home-based care for immobile and elderly persons, reducing their reliance on human caregivers for basic tasks.

Based on the three scenario stories, the NRP R&D team identified two possible extreme cases to build possible scenarios. The first extreme case pertained to the pervasiveness and commercial adoption of the soft robotic applications. A future was envisioned where these scenario stories or use-cases were heavily normalized and interwoven into the everyday processes within the healthcare domain. This first extreme value coincided with the NRP's strategic thrust of mass market adoption in the public and private sectors and would immensely contribute to the country's vision to adopt ubiquitous technology and become a Smart Nation. The second extreme case involved the speed and intensity of advancement in the soft robotic technologies. Like the first, this second extreme value was highly desirable and ideal, significantly shortening the lead time to meet market demand. This extreme case would require an extensive and robust ecosystem involving research institutes and their talent pool, industry-driven roadmaps, investment and funding bodies, and a large measure of coordination among the stakeholders. The team could therefore build scenarios around the degrees of adherence to these two extreme values.

---

15 Kyree Leary, "Georgia Tech's New Prosthetic Arm Enables Amputees to Control Each Individual Finger", December 12, 2017, accessed April 5, 2019, https://futurism.com/georgia-techs-new-prosthetic-arm-enables-amputees-control-individual-finger.

16 Roceso Technologies, "Soft Robotic Exoskeleton Technologies For Rehabilitation And Assistance", accessed April 5, 2019, https://www.roceso.com/.

17 Swiss National Centre of Competence in Research, "Brain Computer Interfaces (BCI)", accessed April 5, 2019, https://nccr-robotics.ch/research-areas/wearable-robotics/brain-computer-interfaces-bci/.

Inspection and maintenance works in constrained environments

In the inspection and maintenance domain, two scenario stories were identified drawing upon the perceptions and ideas on soft robotics technologies surfaced during the previous stages of the workshop. The first scenario story would use soft actuators to conduct the inspection in highly complex mechanical systems, such as aircraft engine turbines. Padded on top of these robotic systems were soft sensors to enhance their ability to diagnose various miniscule parts of a mechanical system for routine maintenance. Rolls-Royce had deployed such soft robotic applications in the inspection and maintenance of its airplane engine turbines. The snake-like robot could worm its way inside an aircraft engine mounted on the wing, saving the days it would take to remove the engine, inspect it and put it back. Of the technologies the company had explored to solve the inefficiency of human inspection and maintenance, Head of Communications at Rolls-Royce Oliver Walker-Jones, declared that this was "the killer one".[18] Its creator, Arnau Garriga Casanovas, highlighted that the robot's use of soft materials had allowed it to be small and agile in the confined spaces of an engine turbine. Besides inspection and maintenance of engine turbines, the snake robot could be deployed for urban uses in escalator and elevator shafts and building facade claddings.

The second scenario that surfaced in the workshop involved the inspection and maintenance of infrastructural systems involving pipes and ducts, especially if the area for inspection was far from the access point of the pipe system or when the pipe system was convoluted. These soft robotic applications would be critical for preventive maintenance. In situations where a pipe leakage or blockage could be detrimental, the soft robots would not only safeguard against adverse outcomes, but also eliminate the need to take apart or cut open a pipe segment, thereby increasing productivity and reducing costs. One such example was Robot Daisy developed in 2017 by the Massachusetts Institute of Technology.[19] Robot Daisy utilized a system of soft sensors to pinpoint water leaks along a piping system as it crossed a compromised segment. Inserted first into an underground piping through a fire hydrant, Robot Daisy floated through the piping system and once retrieved, the computer chip storing all the data in her body would connect to Wi-Fi and download a map of the leaks. The robot allowed for the early detection of leaks, which "could equate to preventing the loss of millions of gallons of water annually," explained Mark Gallager, Director of Engineering and Distribution at the Cambridge, Massachusetts Water Department,

---

18 Jeremy Wagstaff, "Snake on a plane! Don't panic, it's probably just a (soft) robot", June 19, 2017, accessed April 5, 2019, https://www.reuters.com/article/us-tech-robots/snake-on-a-plane-dont-panic-its-probably-just-a-robot-idUSKBN19A0UV.
19 Karen Hao, "A little squishy robot named Daisy is on a quest to save all of our drinking water", September 28, 2017, accessed April 5, 2019, https://qz.com/1085752/an-mit-phd-student-designed-a-soft-robot-named-daisy-to-save-cities-millions-in-water-leaks/.

"[It could also] minimize the damage to infrastructure and the loss of water services to homes and businesses [during a pipe failure]."

Following the narration of the two scenario stories, the NRP R&D team revisited the two extreme cases it had earlier conceived for future scenarios in the healthcare domain. Within the inspection and maintenance domain, the first extreme value of widespread adoption would see an immense variety of manufacturing industries utilizing soft robotics, especially in the aviation industry where complex and large engines were fabricated. These robots would be commonplace in the routine inspection of such systems, replacing the over-reliance on human labor. Next, the second extreme value mirrored that of the healthcare domain, where a high level of coordination and collaboration among stakeholders (including policymakers, research institutes, end-users) would be required for swift development and rollout of emerging soft robotic technologies.

Looking back at the use-case scenarios it had fleshed out, alongside the two extreme cases for each domain's future scenarios, the workshop led the participants to project a research roadmap in the form of a timeline for the realization of each scenario story. The participants forecasted that the healthcare domain would see a swifter realization than the inspection and maintenance domain. See Figure 5.4 for a summary of the scenario stories and their realization timeline.

Next steps

Using the scenario stories as inspiration, the team planned to generate a robotics R&D and commercialization roadmap for selected industries for the next ten years. Two approaches were apparent to the team in seeking technical and industry expertise to develop a comprehensive and holistic roadmap. They could either initiate a grant-call or invite bottom-up proposals.

Initiating a grant call

In the typical grant call, the grantor would make public an invitation for potential applicants to submit proposals that would comply with the scope and eligibility criteria set by the grantor. By having the grant call open to eligible participants, there would be virtually no limit to the number of proposals that the grantor could receive. After the proposal submission deadline, the grantor would exercise its right to select the proposal(s) it deemed the best based on its evaluation criteria. Grant calls were typically aligned to industry and nationwide challenges and opportunities that the grantor had an interest in pursuing.

Figure 5.4: Summary of scenario stories and realization timeline.
Source: Organization document.

The National Research Foundation (NRF) of Singapore, of which the NRP was one of its offices, was prolific in initiating grant calls and awarding grants to deserving researchers and research institutes in Singapore. The most notable was its Competitive Research Programme (CRP) that had seen a significant number of successful grant calls since its inception in April 2007.[20] Each successful proposal was awarded more than S$10 million. As of March 2019, there had been 22 grant calls under the CRP scheme. The Nanyang Technological University (NTU) was a productive research institute that was frequently awarded grants under the CRP. One successful project from NTU named "Nanonets" was led by Professor Subodh Mhaisalkar and his team who focused on novel nanomaterials that would bring new functionalities to applications in green energy systems.[21] Speaking on the assistance of the grant scheme, Professor Mhaisalkar said that it was "indeed an honor to receive the grant from the NRF". Continuing, he said that it was "an acknowledgement that the project proposed by our team [was] of the highest scientific standard and [was] well aligned with the national research agenda."

Should the NRP R&D team opt to initiate grant calls, the potential benefits were twofold. First, as a grant call was regulated by a formalized system of requirements and eligibility criteria, the process of selecting worthy projects would be highly efficient and impartial, ensuring that funds would be disbursed in an optimal manner. There would be little room for dispute since the eligibility and evaluation criteria were spelled out unambiguously. Applicants would need to adhere to strict requirements made known by the grantor. Next, since the grant call was publicly announced as in the case of nationwide open grant calls, the pool of prospective applicants would be significantly wider compared to that of a closed grant call limited to a smaller pool of pre-selected participants for specific reasons. As a result, the likelihood of the team receiving a larger volume and greater diversity of applications would increase.

Not without its limitations, a grant call might ultimately generate too few applications owing to the specificity of its scope and the strictness of its eligibility requirements. This limitation would be most apparent when the pool of prospective applicants was small to begin with, perhaps due to the specificity of the domain or technology. A grant call would be an inefficient approach should a dearth of proposals be received. Another potential drawback to grant calls might be its compromise of quality for quantity. Since the number of possible proposals was virtually unlimited, the relative chance that a single proposal be selected as the best one would be low. This might discourage the best researchers or research institutes from submitting a proposal, thereby depriving the grant call the opportunity to receive high-quality proposals. These researchers or research institutes might prefer

20 National Research Foundation, "Competitive Research Programme", accessed April 5, 2019, https://www.nrf.gov.sg/funding-grants/competitive-research-programme.
21 Nanyang Technological University, "NTU receives S$30 million Competitive Research Programme grants", July 7, 2009, accessed April 5, 2019, http://news.ntu.edu.sg/Pages/NewsDetail.aspx?URL= http://news.ntu.edu.sg/news/Pages/NR2009_Jul07.aspx&Guid=77f3543d-4bcb-4981-9f0b-fa8204699938&Category=News+Releases.

to submit proposals in a closed, bottom-up approach since their proposals would more likely be considered by the grantor than other competing proposals.

The grantor also had to consider the costs associated with the clarification, screening and evaluation of a possible deluge of proposals received. Should this be resource-intensive, the grantor would have to incur high costs in the proposal selection process.

Inviting bottom-up proposals

With extensive information about future scenarios and good knowledge about the experts and their research fields, the grantor could also consider directly inviting the most suitable researchers to submit proposals. Unlike a grant call that would be open to eligible participants, a bottom-up proposal approach would use a closed and exclusive mode of invitation to encourage participation by highly qualified or specialized experts. In the bottom-up proposal approach, the funding body or grantor would strategically select participants, define the problem to be solved, and ultimately select the final solution. Participation would be closed to the extent that the opportunity to submit a proposal would be limited to a pre-determined group of participants due to the limited pool of experts available. An example of a closed and bottom-up approach was conducted by Alessi, an Italian design company of home products. Owing to its focus on unique and post-modern design, it decided to invite a selected group of over 200 known designers to propose new product designs. The curation of this list of designers was derived from Alessi's careful consideration and understanding of the industry's key players.

Having a smaller pool of invited experts would likely mean that each expert's proposal had a higher chance of being thoroughly reviewed and ultimately adopted, thus incentivizing the submission of higher-quality proposals. In instances where the defined problem was specific and required expertise was highly-specialized, and when the pool of prospective participants was understood to be small, an invitation for bottom-up proposals would allow for an effective and efficient receipt of meaningful proposals. Since the selection and definition of the problem was predetermined by the grantor, there should be minimal deviations between the average proposal received and the ideal proposal.

However, this option was not free of its potential drawbacks. Inviting bottom-up proposals was fundamentally risky due to the grantor's pre-selection of the knowledge domain and the invited researchers and research institutes within that domain. Choosing this approach would involve taking on the risk that the identified knowledge domain might not effectively address the problems identified. The success of this option was dependent on the grantor's thorough understanding and good judgment of the invited experts' competence and willingness to contribute.

To increase the likelihood of success in bottom-up proposals, the grantor had to consider several factors. First, having established relationships and networks with industry experts would facilitate the grantor's endeavor to elicit proposals from them since this mode of collaboration depended on informal relationships rather than a rigid and structured system. Further, the legitimacy and clout of the grantor would enable them to productively invite and receive proposals from industry experts. Had the grantor not garnered institutional legitimacy and industry-backing, the process of inviting bottom-up proposals would be comparatively more difficult.

Moving forward

As Ooi's team deliberated on the grant call approach and the bottom-up proposal method, it knew that it had to make a decision soon on which path to take.

Learning objectives

This case aims to highlight the following:
- Importance of the imagination phase of SFM to generate future visions and scenarios.
- Process of scenario development to chart the future directions of an organization and its related industries.
- Importance of identifying the relevant stakeholders and using the appropriate platforms to engage them so as to understand their perception and mental models.
- Purpose and usefulness of storytelling in developing future scenarios and capturing their impact and uncertainty.
- A range of collaboration strategies that vary by participation level and hierarchy degree are available for organizations to co-create future value.
- Importance and drawbacks of community participation and partnerships involved in co-creation.

Sarah Cheah

6 Technology Management: Building and Validating Roadmaps

On April 9, 2019, the R&D team headed by Edmund Ooi of the National Robotics Programme (NRP) Office had completed over ten months of R&D roadmapping project in collaboration with Professor Sarah Cheah of the National University of Singapore (NUS) Business School. The project had conducted horizon scanning, patent analysis, literature review and scenario building before generating technology/R&D roadmaps in three key areas: (a) robotic end-effectors with integrated perception (or gripper robotics), (b) autonomous vehicles with sensor fusion and (c) on-chip Light Detection and Ranging (LiDAR) system for autonomous robotics. Building on these technology/R&D roadmaps, integrated roadmaps were also developed for two target domains – healthcare and environment. The project team went on to validate these roadmaps through a Delphi survey involving 70 industry and technology experts.[1] The survey had several findings.

First, in line with expectations, autonomous vehicles were found to have the greatest impact for social and citizen well-being, while LiDAR and gripper robotics had that for industry and economic growth. Second, as the team had postulated, Singapore's strongest competence in gripper robotics, LiDAR and autonomous vehicles was evident in its availability of funding, infrastructure and design/engineering know-how, respectively. Third, LiDAR and autonomous vehicles were found to have similar forecasted realization as anticipated due to their complementarity with each other. However, widespread use for gripper robotics was projected to take a longer time than that of LiDAR and autonomous vehicles, which went counter to the NRP R&D team's understanding that the latter would take a longer time due to the more stringent safety regulations imposed by the local land transport authority.

As Ooi scrutinized the roadmap recommendations and Delphi results, he knew that gripper robotics would be important based on his earlier review of the patent analysis and literature review findings. However, he needed some confirmation about further investment in LiDAR and autonomous vehicles. Given limited time and resources, which technology should his team focus on: LiDAR or autonomous vehicles?

---

1 Delphi study was a foresight method where questionnaires about certain trends or phenomena were sent to a group of experts more than once, with results being shared with the participants after each round, with the objective of generating consensus.

---

https://doi.org/10.1515/9783110672916-006

Building roadmaps

Nearing the close of 2017, Ooi's team launched a roadmappping study in collaboration with Cheah. The roadmap they sought to develop would enable identification of key research areas so that future market demand could be forecasted, and resources be channeled into optimal areas to meet demand in a timely manner. Adopting the methodology of roadmapping,[2] the project team constructed the roadmap in sequential phases: (a) horizon scanning, (b) patent analysis and literature review, (c) technology/R&D roadmapping and (d) integrated roadmapping.

Horizon scanning

In the first quarter of 2018, the project team scanned the horizon for market drivers in the two key domains of healthcare and environment, allowing them to flesh out the first band of the roadmap that comprised the market drivers.

In the healthcare domain, whose global industry was slated to generate around US$1.8 billion revenue in 2017 and 2018 with a short-term annual growth rate of about five per cent, the Asia-Pacific region commanded the second largest global market share, growing at a rate of 11 per cent. In the context of Singapore, three key market drivers were surfaced. They were (a) emerging consumer power, (b) radical cost escalation and (c) industry structure transformation. As consumers grew accustomed to the digitalization of services in general, it was expected that this would translate into the healthcare industry too. In fact, the digitalization of clinical operations was expected to generate global financial potential of up to US$155 billion. Costs escalated in part due to the aging population in Singapore, who were four times more likely to be hospitalized than the younger population. At the same time, a rise in chronic and infectious diseases as demonstrated by the increasing frequency of visits to primary care facilities for these diseases contributed to radical cost escalation.

In the environment domain, markets were driven by widespread and rapid urbanization in Singapore. With 100 per cent of its total population living in urban areas, Singapore's projected rate of change of the size of its urban population from 2015 at 5.54 million to 2020 was 1.39 per cent. Further, the National Environment Agency of Singapore had cited that there was a growing demand of waste recycling services in Singapore, ranging from general waste to food waste. The recycling rate

---

2 Phaal, Robert, Clare J.P. Farrukh, and David R. Probert. "Technology Roadmapping – A Planning Framework for Evolution and Revolution." Technological Forecasting and Social Change, 71, no. 1–2 (2004): 5–26. doi:10.1016/s0040-1625(03)00072-6.

for the latter was 16 per cent in 2017 and slated to continue rising.[3] The three market drivers identified were (a) urbanization, (b) slow workforce growth, and an (c) aging population.

Following from these market drivers, the team identified the key business sectors within that domain which were influenced by the earlier market drivers. In the healthcare domain, the most prominent business sector that was predicted to emerge was smart hospitals. These advanced medical institutions would focus on three aspects: (a) operational efficiency, (b) clinical excellence and (c) patient centricity. In validation of their growing ubiquity, a Frost & Sullivan report cited that by 2025, 10 per cent of hospitals worldwide would become or have started implementations to become smart hospitals. On the environment front, two key business sectors were identified as (a) outdoor cleaning and (b) waste management. The key business sectors made up the second band of the integrated industry roadmap.

Finally, the key applications of robotics technologies made up for the third band of the integrated industry roadmap. In the healthcare domain, three key applications were identified: (a) logistic management and professional indoor cleaning for operational efficiency, (b) surgical robots for clinical excellence and (c) telemedicine and rehabilitative robots for patient centricity. For the environment domain, the key applications were: (a) professional outdoor cleaning and (b) waste collection and waste recycling.

A summary of the market drivers, key business sectors and applications for both the healthcare and environment domains could be found in Figure 6.1.

Patent analysis and literature review

From the start of the second quarter of 2018, the project team conducted patent analysis and literature review on the key research areas. From the findings, Ooi and his team identified not only the key industry players who were top patent assignees of specific research areas, but also opportunities for robotics technologies. For example, the team discovered new commercial opportunities for gripper technology in the area of handling non-standardized items. This discovery validated their support of companies that utilized advanced gripper technology to meet the underserved market. One such company that seized the opportunity was a Singapore-based gripper company Hand Plus Robotics founded in July 2018.[4] In a similar way, strong international players such as cleaning robot company iRobot Inc. were identified from the patent analysis as potential partners to companies with complementary competencies such as

---

3 National Environment Agency, "Waste Statistics and Overall Recycling", accessed March 20, 2019, http://www.nea.gov.sg/energy-waste/waste-management/waste-statistics-and-overall-recycling.
4 Hand Plus Robotics, "About Us", accessed March 27, 2019, http://www.handplusrobotics.com/Home.php#AboutUs.

Market Driver - Healthcare

Radical cost escalation

Industry structure transformation

Emerging consumer power

Key Business Sectors

Operational efficiency

Clinical excellence

Patient centricity

Applications

Logistic management

Surgical robots

Telemedicine

Professional cleaning (indoor)

Rehabilitative robots

Market Driver - Environment

Urbanization

Slow workforce growth

Aging population

Key Business Sectors

Cleaning

Waste management

Applications

Professional cleaning (outdoor)

Waste collection

Waste recycling

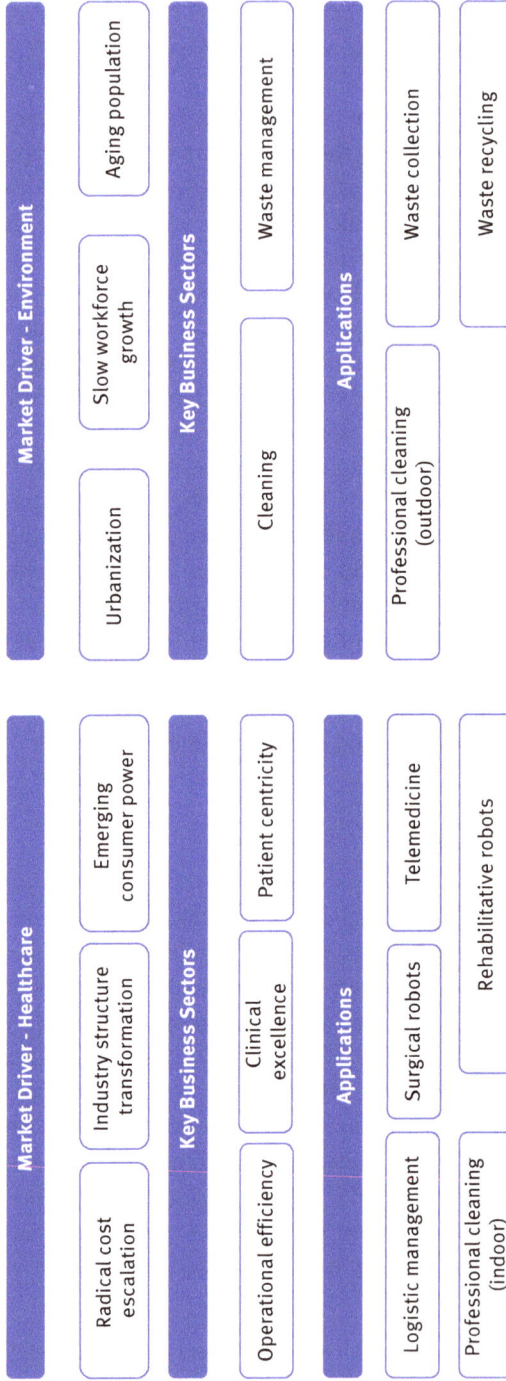

Figure 6.1: Market drivers, key business sectors and applications from horizon scanning.
Source: Author's research and analysis.

the Singapore-based company LionsBot that offered cleaning robots.[5] Visiting regional trade shows also proved crucial in tracking technology development in non-English speaking countries. Patent findings supplemented by such visits had allowed the project to identify resources and capabilities for new technologies. For example, the resources and capabilities required for LiDAR technology included material science engineering and micro-electronics system engineering.

Based on the literature review and patent analysis, the project team found that service mobile robots that utilized indoor and outdoor autonomous vehicles had five levels of autonomy, while focusing on the three highest levels for building the technology roadmap. These were "Highly Autonomous", "Fully-Autonomous", and "Cooperative". As an illustration, the highest level of autonomy, "Cooperative", encompassed mobile service robots that could adapt to varied, uncertain and complex environments and navigate in unstructured and unpredictable environments. Beyond service mobile robots, levels of autonomy were identified for aerial robots too. Three levels were identified, with the highest level enabling the aerial service robot to operate free from human intervention. For each of these levels of autonomy for both service mobile and aerial robots, the corresponding technology levels and R&D program were mapped, ranging from T1 to T12 and R1 to R12, respectively. At the lowest technology level of T1, the robot was assisted and guided by markers, beacons and floor grids, as it was not capable of autonomous obstacle avoidance and hence unsafe to operate in the same space as humans. At the highest level of T12 technology, the robot would be fully autonomous without the need for human operation. Similarly, in the lowest level of R1 research, the research focused on the improvement of indoor and outdoor navigation capabilities. At the highest level of R12 research, the research would focus on advanced algorithms for perception, mapping, localization and planning in 3D environments. The resources and capabilities required for autonomous vehicle technology included image processing, signal processing, machine and deep learning, neural networks, natural language processing, artificial intelligence (AI) visual odometry and robot operating system.

Since LiDAR technology was closely related and complementary to autonomous vehicle technology, technology levels for pure solid-state LiDAR were identified from T13 to T15. T13 was defined as technology capabilities on Optical Phased Array based Pure Solid-State LiDAR with data processing system, while T15 as technology capabilities on Application Specific LiDARs based on range, resolution and cost. The related R&D programs were correspondingly defined from R13 to R15 for the development of LiDAR technology. The resources and capabilities required for LiDAR comprised material science, micro-electronics systems, data analytics, process integration, embedded system programming, laser/optical physics, signal processing conditioning, as well as lens physics.

---

5 LionsBot, "About Us – Robotics for better living", accessed March 25, 2019, https://www.lionsbot.com/about-us/.

Technology/R&D roadmapping

The technology/R&D roadmap for autonomous vehicle and LiDAR technologies were generated by mapping and linking T1 to T15, R1 to R15, as well as resources and capabilities in three bands: technology roadmap, R&D programs and resources/capabilities. See Figure 6.2 for the technology/R&D roadmap of autonomous vehicles and LiDAR.

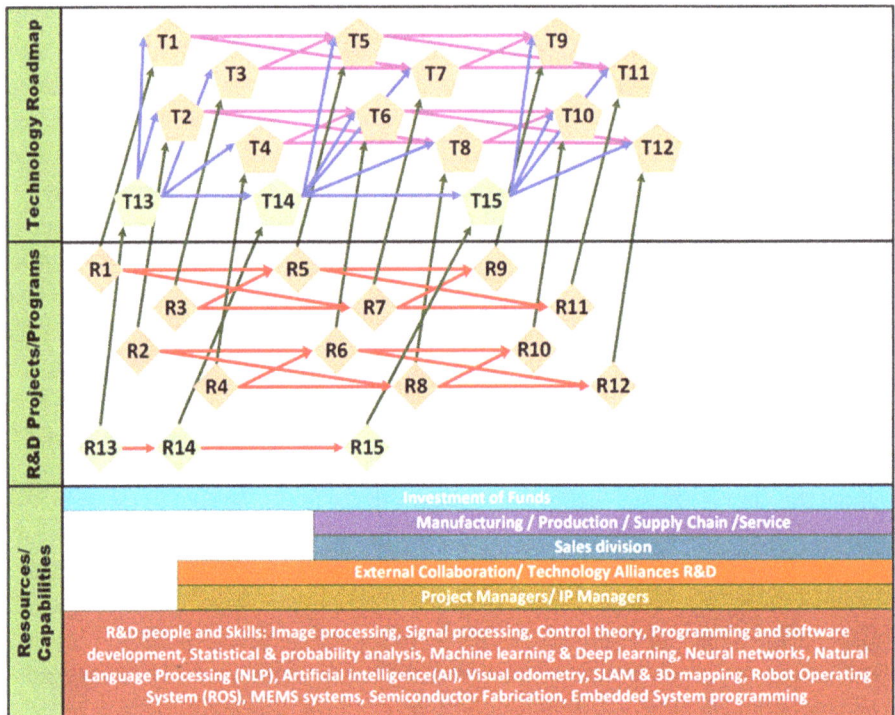

Figure 6.2: Technology/R&D roadmap for autonomous navigation/LiDAR technologies.
Source: Author's research and analysis.

The project team repeated the same process of roadmap generation for gripper technology, supported by the complementary technologies of computer vision and tactile skin. Beginning with grippers, four technology levels were identified from T1 to T4, with the highest level constituting an advanced gripper equipped with advanced AI. Four related R&D programs were identified from R1 to R4, with its highest level pertaining to research that focused on advanced AI development and integration for autonomous gripping. As computer vision was highly complementary to a robotic gripper's capabilities, four technology levels from T5 to T8 were likewise identified. Similar to the highest technology level for grippers, that for computer vision was also AI-integrated and completely free from human intervention in its operation. Four R&D programs from R5 to R8 were identified for computer vision, with its highest level similarly focusing on advanced AI development and integration. The final supporting technology of a robotic gripper was its tactile skin that would provide sensing capabilities to a gripper. Four technology levels were identified again from T9 to T12, with its most advanced form mimicking human skin as closely as possible, integrated with AI and computer vision. In the same fashion as gripper and computer vision technology, four related R&D programs from R9 to R12 were identified. To integrate gripper, computer vision and AI, three grasping framework solution levels were identified from T13 to T15, with corresponding R&D programs from R13 to R15. See Figure 6.3 for the technology/R&D roadmap with resources and capabilities required for the development of grasping framework solutions integrating gripper, computer vision and AI technologies.

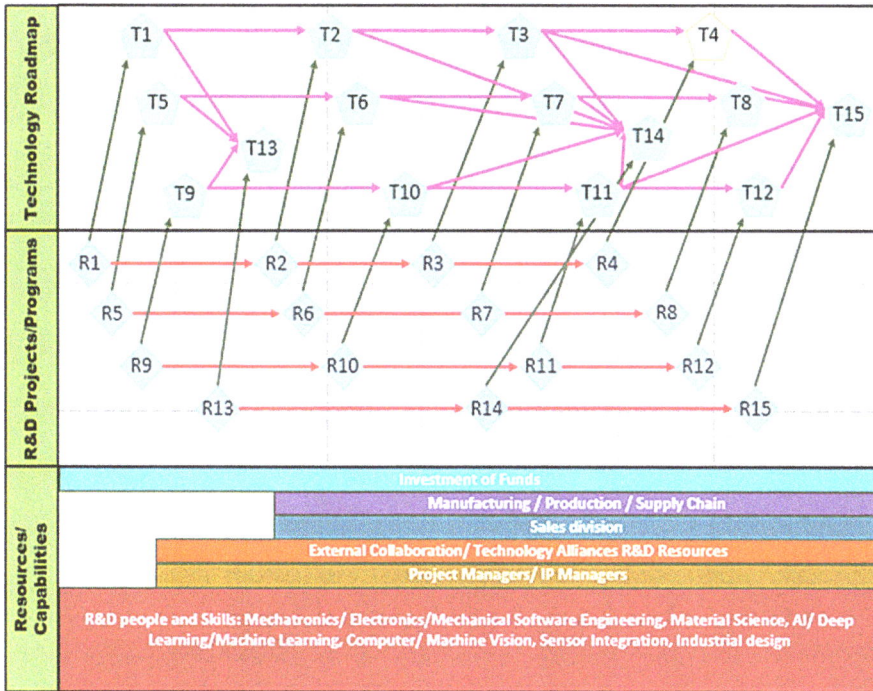

Figure 6.3: Technology/R&D roadmap for gripper/computer vision/AI technologies.
Source: Author's research and analysis.

Integrated roadmapping

By the end of second quarter 2018, the project team had gathered information for all the six bands that were required for integrated roadmapping for target domains – healthcare and environment. In the healthcare domain, an integrated roadmap was generated for care delivery and consumer engagement by combining market drivers, key business sectors, and applications for healthcare from horizon scanning in Figure 6.1 to form the first three bands. The integrated roadmap also combined the technology/R&D roadmap for autonomous vehicle/LiDAR technologies from literature review/patent analysis in Figure 6.2 and that for gripper/computer vision/AI technologies in Figure 6.3.

Roadmapping was an important strategic foresight tool for identifying emergent market and technology trends, and formulating long-range plans for resource allocation to exploit the opportunities systematically. However, the volatility, uncertainty and complexity of the external environment might render the roadmap irrelevant or obsolete. While some might advocate the need for a more dynamic roadmap to respond to external turbulences, others would find it too onerous to update the roadmap frequently. Ooi acknowledged this limitation, citing that "sometimes it becomes irrelevant because technology can change very fast". As an example, he highlighted that LiDAR capabilities became inferior to camera and computer vision that had improved over time to be able to detect objects as sharply as the human eye. It might no longer be necessary to develop LiDAR technology, thereby potentially rendering one area of the roadmap retrospectively irrelevant. On the other hand, as the NRP R&D team executed trajectories that deviated over time from the pathways suggested by the roadmap, the roadmap then became something that the team would refer to retroactively, rather than as a guide for future development. Ooi cautioned that "you don't want to [obstinately] follow the LiDAR trajectory [and] end up [realizing] it doesn't work out."

Validating roadmaps with Delphi survey

With the integrated roadmaps fleshed out, it would be important to validate them. The Delphi method was a forecasting tool that was frequently used to seek consensus among experts on certain trends or trajectories. It had been employed in a wide variety of fields, ranging from national foresight studies on science and technology to corporate strategic foresight. One such study in Taiwan had integrated the Delphi survey method alongside scenario analysis to forecast the development of organic light-emitting diode televisions.[6]

In the third quarter of 2018, the project team developed a survey questionnaire comprising statements that would depict the technology trajectory and market

---

6 Hung, Chih-Young, Wen-Yee Lee, and Ding-Shan Wang. "Strategic foresight using a modified Delphi with end-user participation: A case study of the iPad's impact on Taiwan's PC ecosystem." Technological Forecasting and Social Change 80, no. 3 (2013): 485–497.

trends captured in the integrated roadmaps. The questionnaire asked about the local impact, competence and forecasted realization time for each of the three key technology areas – gripper robotics, LiDAR and autonomous vehicles. Four statements were generated for each technology after an initial round of interviews in April 2018 with relevant technology-specific experts. Pegged to each of these statements were three questions.

The first of the three probed for why the statement would greatly influence Singapore. Available responses included "social and citizen well-being" and "industry/economic growth". The second question asked respondents to identify Singapore's strongest competence related to that statement, including responses such as "availability of funding", "infrastructure" and "skilled labor force." The final question asked respondents to forecast the time of realization of this statement in Singapore. Respondents had to identify a specific year for the achievement of four milestones for the statement's technology trend: its R&D development, first successful demonstration, commercialization and widespread use.

The project team launched the Delphi survey in the final quarter of 2018 to seek out and tap on the judgments of expert opinions regarding the possible future realities that the integrated roadmap suggested. The experts' responses were then compiled and shared with the experts in a controlled manner to elicit further responses about the results. The participants were invited to participate more than once so as to foster convergence of results and build consensus.

Delphi survey results

By the end of November 2018, the Delphi survey results had taken meaningful shape, having come from a diverse range of industry experts across the three robotic technologies. The results yielded comparative insights that allowed Ooi and his team to validate and further refine their understanding of the trajectories of grippers, LiDAR, and autonomous vehicles in Singapore.

On the first question that pertained to the most important reason for the stated technology to demonstrate high impact in Singapore, it was found that 42 per cent respondents felt autonomous vehicles would demonstrate the largest impact on social and citizen well-being. LiDAR technology was found to pose the greatest impact for industry and economic growth (74 per cent) among other factors. Finally, the impact of gripper robotics on industry and economic growth (56 per cent) was found to be larger than that for social and citizen well-being (37 per cent). These results resonated with the NRP R&D team's expectations since they knew that autonomous vehicles were often associated with humans of menial tasks at the workplace or home to improve well-being while gripper robotics with performing tasks of picking and placing objects for patients in homes.

The second question pertained to Singapore's strongest competence in the three technologies, relative to the world. Among gripper robotics, 31 per cent of respondents identified Singapore's availability of funding as its greatest source of competence. For LiDAR technology, 27 per cent of respondents identified infrastructure as Singapore's key competence. Finally, 24 per cent of respondents identified design and engineering know-how as the primary competence to drive the future development of autonomous vehicles. The team found these results to be in line with their expectations, since very few countries besides Singapore invested in the development of gripper robotics for handling non-standard items. On the other hand, there had been extensive funding by both public and private sectors outside Singapore on the other two areas – LiDAR and autonomous vehicles. The local competence on infrastructure was rated the highest for LiDAR as the country had provided many infrastructural facilities for prototyping and pilot-testing to support its deployment. The competence for design/engineering know-how for autonomous vehicles was rated the strongest as the aesthetic aspects of such vehicles were regarded as important for their adoption by end users across healthcare and other sectors.

The third and final question pertained to respondents' expectation for the realization of each technology's statements in Singapore. Across the board, gripper robotics was found to have the slowest time of realization, with its eventual "widespread use year" coming slightly after 2026, as opposed to autonomous vehicles and LiDAR technology that respondents predicted to come slightly after 2025. The timelines of realization for autonomous vehicles and LiDAR technology were very similar. Taking stock of these results, Ooi opined that the forecasted time of realization for the first three phases (R&D development, first successful demonstration and commercialization) was in line with the team's expectations for all three technologies, where autonomous vehicles and LiDAR had been projected to have shorter realization time than grippers since innovation efforts had been more intense from R&D to commercialization on the former two technologies for their commercial potential than the latter. However, Ooi predicted that the achievement of widespread use should have been much longer for these two technologies as opposed to gripper robotics because applications of the former two technologies had to satisfy various government regulations regarding land transport (Ministry of Health and Land Transport Authority), reliability (National Environment Agency), ethics, and the liability of insurance companies. The team surmised that the realization of gripper robotics' widespread use, on the other hand, should have taken a shorter time than the former two technologies due to fewer governmental restrictions.

Prioritizing resource allocation

With results and insights from the Delphi survey, the NRP R&D team knew that gripper robotics would continue to be a strategic area for capability development, as suggested by the earlier patent analysis and literature review findings. However, Ooi needed some confirmation about further investment in LiDAR and autonomous vehicles. Given limited time and resources, which technology should the team accord the higher priority for resource allocation: LiDAR or autonomous vehicles?

LiDAR

Many international players had been attracted to the rapid expansion and growth of the global LiDAR market that was predicted to garner US$921.2 million by 2022,[7] growing at a considerable compound annual growth rate (CAGR) of 18.5 per cent from the period of 2016 to 2022. The state of the technology had been making improvements worldwide, with LiDAR systems' image resolution and data processing capabilities driving the growth of their market. The growth of complementary industries was also driving demand for LiDAR to augment technologies within the fields of meteorology, cartography, urban planning, exploration, driverless cars, advanced driver assistance systems (ADAS), engineering and corridor mapping.[8] According to Market Research Gazette, the global LiDAR market for driverless cars and ADAS was envisaged to grow at an aggressive pace in the future. ABI Research forecasted in 2018 that by 2025 there would be eight million autonomous vehicles with level three or higher autonomy.[9]

Positioned well within the global LiDAR market, the Asia-Pacific region was forecasted to sport the highest CAGR out of all regions, growing at a pace of 25 per cent during the forecast 2016 to 2022 period, amassing a total value of US$205.6 million by 2022 and accounting for more than 22 per cent of global value.[10] Singapore, in

---

7 Allied Market Research, "LiDAR Market by Product Type, Application, Components and End User – Global Opportunity Analysis and Industry Forecast, 2015 – 2022", April 2016, accessed April 9, 2019, https://www.alliedmarketresearch.com/lidar-market.

8 Market Research Gazette, "LiDAR Market to Witness a Pronounce Growth During 2017 to 2025", April 8, 2019, accessed April 9, 2019, https://amarketresearchgazette.com/lidar-market-to-witness-a-pronounce-growth-during-2017-to-2025/.

9 ABI Research, "ABI Research Forecasts 8 Million Vehicles to Ship with SAE Level 3, 4 and 5 Autonomous Technology in 2025", April 17, 2018, accessed April 9, 2019, https://www.abire search.com/press/abi-research-forecasts-8-million-vehicles-ship-sae-level-3-4-and-5-autonomous-technology-2025/.

10 Markets and Markets, "LiDAR Market worth 1,809.5 Million USD by 2023", May 2018, accessed April 9, 2019, https://www.marketsandmarkets.com/PressReleases/lidar.asp.

particular, was a likely contender in reaping the benefits of its strategic position in Southeast Asia as the demand for 3D imaging had been increasing among emerging countries in the region due to its high adoption in corridor mapping, healthcare and forest zone management applications. As these emerging Southeast Asian nations developed their infrastructural capabilities, such as planning and monitoring activities related to roadways, railways, cities and forest management among others, commercial and government sectors within the region were likely to drive the demand for LiDAR technology in the region. The sum of these factors indicated to Ooi's team that there was indeed aggressive future demand and growth prospects for the LiDAR industry, and developing LiDAR capabilities in Singapore would allow local companies to benefit from this global demand.

The team had to consider the challenges of pursuing LiDAR technology due to several factors. First, the global market for LiDAR seemed very saturated, with numerous capable players in the American, European, and Asia-Pacific regions vying for a dominant global position. Furthermore, a MarketsandMarkets report forecasted the Asia-Pacific region to exhibit the highest rate of growth between 2019 and 2023 among all global competition, signaling the intensity and congestion of the regional market that Singaporean capabilities would need to stack up against. Beyond the region, there was an abundance of dominant players in the LiDAR market such as Velodyne LiDAR Inc. and LeddarTech.

Velodyne LiDAR Inc. was the recognized global leader in LiDAR technology, developing full 360-degree environmental view for use in autonomous vehicles, industrial equipment, 3D mapping and surveillance functions. Helmed by CEO David Hall, Velodyne had asserted its dominance in the LiDAR market by reaching its US$500 million milestone in 2019, with sales of 30,000 units of laser LiDAR sensors to a multitude of self-driving car programs since 2007.[11] Velodyne was no stranger to constant innovation, as it unveiled its latest product, the VLS-128 in January 2019, which it boasted to be "perfect for Level 4–5 autonomy" – nearly at the apex technological advancement in autonomous vehicles.[12] The company's president, Mike Jellen, claimed that its new product was "the best LiDAR sensor on the planet", offering high-resolution imaging that was unrivaled by competitors. Also at the forefront of LiDAR technology was the Canadian company LeddarTech. It had developed a proprietary LiDAR technology called Leddar that could detect, locate and measure objects, including liquids and people, in a given field of view. They had developed LeddarCore, the LiDAR industry's

---

11 Alan Ohnsman, "Velodyne's Godfather Of Laser Sensors Hits $500 Million Milestone, Sets His Sights On Safer Self-Driving Cars", March 22, 2019, accessed March 27, 2019, https://www.forbes.com/sites/alanohnsman/2019/03/22/velodynes-godfather-of-laser-sensors-hits-500-million-milestone-sets-his-sights-on-safer-self-driving-cars/#5ef250446035.

12 Philip E. Ross, "Velodyne Unveils Monster Lidar With 128 Laser Beams", November 28, 2017, accessed March 27, 2019, https://spectrum.ieee.org/cars-that-think/transportation/sensors/velodyne-unveils-monster-lidar-with-128-laser-beams.

first 3D solid-state LiDAR system-on-chip (SoC), enabling the rapid production of 3D solid-state LiDARs (SSLs) for the automotive industry. In further support of LeddarTech's dominance as an industry innovator, the company released production samples of its latest development, the LeddarCore LC2 SoC in January 2019.[13]

The NRP R&D team predicted that the state of the market surrounding LiDAR technology might disincentivize them to prioritize the development of this technology. They were concerned that the market was too congested with strong rivals, and that this would raise the barriers to entry and significantly limit the potential opportunities that a new venture might reap.

A challenge that would result from this congested market space was the attraction of local expertise to multinational corporations abroad. The team recounted its previous experiences building LiDAR capabilities in local public research institutes, only to have them be scouted and hired by dominant multinational corporations who possessed the financial bandwidth to provide more attractive remunerations. With the inability to retain manpower in local public research institutes, the team faced one considerable obstacle to the decision of prioritizing LiDAR technology in Singapore.

Indoor autonomous navigation

Although the autonomous vehicle market was expected to grow from US$2.2 billion in 2018 to US$13.5 billion by 2030 at a CAGR of 16.19 per cent, the team identified a gap that the market currently did not serve extensively.[14] Most players on the market focused on sensing capabilities, but navigational capabilities were surmised as underserved. At its current state, there were many functions that service robots were not able to perform, such as navigating complex and dynamic human environments. Since the team had earlier chosen to focus on the healthcare domain in Singapore, and most notably the business sectors surrounding smart hospitals, navigational capabilities of autonomous service robots were deemed essential. It was on this note that the team chose to focus on the specific subdomain of indoor autonomous navigation. Reflecting on the technology's current limitations, Ooi mentioned that "there are a lot of needs which robots currently cannot perform and that severely limits

---

13 Globe Newswire, "LeddarTech Delivers Production Samples of the LeddarCore LCA2 System-on-Chip for Mass-Market Automotive LiDARs", January 7, 2019, accessed March 27, 2019, https://www.globenewswire.com/news-release/2019/01/07/1680924/0/en/LeddarTech-Delivers-Production-Samples-of-the-LeddarCore-LCA2-System-on-Chip-for-Mass-Market-Automotive-LiDARs.html.

14 Research and Markets, "$13.5 Billion Autonomous Navigation Market by Solution, Platform, Application and Region – Global Forecast to 2030", March 28, 2019, accessed April 9, 2019, https://www.globenewswire.com/news-release/2019/03/28/1781053/0/en/13-5-Billion-Autonomous-Navigation-Market-by-Solution-Platform-Application-and-Region-Global-Forecast-to-2030.html.

[their] usability". Continuing, he admitted that "there [are] a lot of limited [uses] if you have incapable indoor navigation." Although the autonomous vehicle market was strong especially in its outdoor and automotive applications as in Japan, Korea, the United States, and countries in the European Union, Ooi observed, "a lot of countries still overlook [indoor autonomous navigation], or rather it's not a key priority." This therefore opened many opportunities for such capabilities to fill the gap in the market, thus driving support for the decision to prioritize the development of this technology.

One major challenge to autonomous vehicles was the complications surrounding robo-ethics and AI ethics. There existed an advent of service robots increasingly entering the human world, with 12 million service robots in operation around the world in 2017 and an expected increase as reported by the Foundation for Responsible Robotics.[15] The pervading integration of robotics in human society would therefore, necessitate the rise of ethical codes and regulations surrounding their development and use. The first instance of a codified international standard was developed in September 2016 called BS 8611, presented at a conference in Oxford, United Kingdom.[16] A committee of scientists, academics, philosophers, ethicists, and users had developed the standard which was intended for use by robot and robotic device designers and managers. As a growing number of such regulations and standards entered the global market of service robotics and AI, stakeholders in the ecosystem would gradually need to adapt to the changes and uncertainties they might bring.

Ooi reflected that as of 2017, robo-ethics in Singapore did not exist, but was open to the idea that they should be introduced in the near future. Noting the difficulty of implementing ethical codes surrounding robotics, Ooi found "it's hard to configure" and based on strict binaries, leaving little room for in-betweenness. There would be challenges importing ethical codes and legislative frameworks from Western countries, due to the cultural differences with Asia and Singapore. "They could be very different" Ooi mused cautiously.

With the opportunities and limitations identified from integrated roadmapping and insights gained from the Delphi survey, the Ooi's team reflected on the viability of prioritizing the development of LiDAR versus autonomous vehicle capabilities in Singapore.

---

15 Medium, "Rethinking Ethics in the Robotic Age", October 17, 2018, accessed April 9, 2019, https://medium.com/@mitpress/rethinking-ethics-in-the-robotic-age-2a78ea238ba2.
16 Alice Matthews, "How to ethically design your robot", November 1, 2016, accessed April 9, 2019, https://www.electronicspecifier.com/robotics/how-to-ethically-design-your-robot.

Learning objectives

This case discusses the challenges of technology management and illustrates the following:
- Importance of the integration phase of SFM and use of Delphi techniques to analyze and prioritize investment options.
- Relevance of the interpretation phase of SFM and application of roadmapping method to formulate strategies.
- Holistic integration of market drivers, key business sectors and applications from horizon scanning with technologies, R&D programs, resources and capabilities from technology insight to generate integrated roadmaps for future positioning in the target market.
- Application of Delphi surveys to validate roadmaps and prioritize resource allocation for future roadmap implementation.

Sarah Cheah and Saiteja Pattalachinti

7 Commercialization Strategy with Quality Function Deployment

On April 12, 2019, Edmund Ooi stood at his office window, staring at the high-rise buildings outside, home to many technology titans and startups at One North, Singapore. As the Head of the R&D team of the National Robotics Programme Office (NRP) for the past two years, Ooi had reviewed many R&D proposals that were submitted by the researchers of public research institutes and university research centers in response to its grant calls on key areas of robotics research.[1] These proposals were evaluated in three primary aspects: (a) ability to meet national needs, (b) ability to solve manpower shortage and (c) ability to address aging population issues. For those that met these criteria, grants would be awarded for their project implementation with the eventual goal of having their research commercialized and deployed into innovative products and services.

Looking at the slate of projects that had been approved to date, Ooi was heartened that some had successfully completed with patents granted and licensed to existing companies or even to spin-offs founded by the research team. Others were still in the development phase and exploring possible pathways to commercialize into product or service applications. One such project involved the development of end-effector technology integrated with computer vision. End-effectors or grippers referred to the last link of a robot that was designed to interact with the environment, such as picking and placing objects at specific locations. They were mainly used for industrial purposes to pick and place standard-sized objects in a controlled environment. For the past few years, the technology had improved and had been introduced to operate more complex tasks such as performing surgeries as surgical robots.

With advances in emerging technologies such as artificial intelligence (AI), tactile sensing, machine learning and computer vision, the functions of a gripper could be significantly enhanced by incorporating them to guide its grasping strategy. Computer vision, in particular, had been forecast by market analysts to have the potential to drive future innovation in the field of patient engagement and

---

[1] In the typical grant call, the grantor would make public an invitation for potential applicants to submit proposals that would comply with the scope and eligibility criteria set by the grantor.

Note: The author(s) wrote this case solely to provide material for class discussion. The author(s) do not intend to illustrate either effective or ineffective handling of a managerial situation. The author(s) may have disguised certain names and other identifying information to protect confidentiality.

https://doi.org/10.1515/9783110672916-007

social/humanoid robots.[2] The gripper technology with computer vision would stand out in a market flooded with grippers that could only handle certain standard-sized objects in a pre-determined fashion, but lacked flexibility and sensing ability to work in a complex environment. While the gripper technology with computer vision seemed promising, Ooi's team pondered over which commercialization pathway would be the best option for the gripper technology with computer vision.

First, there was the option of licensing the intellectual property (IP), wherein the research institute owning the patent (a form of IP) could grant the commercial rights of the IP to an existing company in exchange for a fee and royalty. Second, the team could consider R&D collaboration where the research institute owning the patent would collaborate with a partner organization to jointly develop the technology to improve its technology readiness level before commercializing it into products and services. The third possible pathway could be a spin-off, in which a member of the researcher team working on the technology would form a new, independent, legal entity to license the IP from the parent research institute for commercialization. Each of these three options had its merits and limitations.

The team had to decide soon as the project completion date loomed near. Should the technology be licensed in its current state to existing companies? Or should it be developed further in research collaboration with other partners to improve the technology readiness level and enhance the chances of its commercial adoption? Or should it support the spin-off by the research team member who might be more motivated but less established than existing companies to commercialize the technology?

'Pick and Place' industry

'Pick and Place' comprised primary handling and case packing.[3] Primary handling constituted putting individual pieces of product into a tray or carton. The type of robot most suited for an application depended on the speed required, payload and other factors. Only one type of robot could be used for a specific job. However, there were borderline applications where more than one type could be used, and the end user had to prioritize the factors.

---

2 Frost & Sullivan. "Innovations in Computer Vision Applications Powered by AI, Harnessing Emerging Business Opportunities Through Visual Intelligence". TechVision Analysis. Report. 2017. Accessed April 15, 2019.

3 Robotics Industries Association, "Pick-and-Place Applications for Robots." *Robotics Online.* December 04, 2011. Accessed April 04, 2019. https://www.robotics.org/content-detail.cfm/ Industrial-Robotics-Industry-Insights/Pick-and-Place-Applications-for-Robots/content_id/2504.

With fast advances in the gripper technology, improvements in payload capacity, sizes, motion control and hardware were evident. Coupled with the introduction of machine learning, computer vision and tactile sensing, this industry was set to grow rapidly. Valued at US$2,471 million in 2016, the packaging robots market was expected to reach US$4,649 million by 2023,[4] growing at the compound annual growth rate (CAGR) of 9.6 percent from 2017 to 2023.[5] Asia-Pacific was expected to dominate the market throughout the forecast period. This was attributed to heavy investment by consumer products and food and beverage industry players in automation. China was the major shareholder in the Asia-Pacific packaging robot industry, accounting for around 45.6 percent share in 2016.[6]

Pick and place robots gained popularity and were anticipated to grow the fastest during the forecast period. These robot systems were flexible and could be easily programmed. In addition, these systems improved product quality and cycle time because of consistent processing. Hence, these robotic systems were projected to grow at a CAGR of 11.4 percent by 2023.[7]

Among the major industry verticals, the packaging robots found widespread usage in the food and beverage industry, which accounted for more than 35 percent share in 2016 owing to increased order volume of fresh food and beverage products. This segment was estimated to witness significant growth during the forecast period due to improving production processes, lowering labor intensity and timely delivery of materials.

A MarketsandMarkets report on industrial robotics market identified the major players in this industry to be ABB Limited, FANUC Corporation, Kawasaki Heavy

---

4 "Packaging Robots Market Is Expected to Reach $4,649 Million, Globally, by 2023." Allied Market Research. Accessed April 04, 2019. https://www.alliedmarketresearch.com/press-release/packaging-robots-market.html.
5 Loomba, Smriti. "Packaging Robots Market by Gripper Type (Claw, Clamp, Vacuum and Others), Application (Picking & Placing, Packing and Palletizing) and End User (Food & Beverage, Pharmaceutical, Logistics, Consumer Products, Logistics and Others) – Global Opportunity Analysis and Industry Forecast, 2017–2023." Allied Market Research. May 2017. Accessed April 05, 2019. https://www.alliedmarketresearch.com/packaging-robots-market.
6 Loomba, Smriti. "Packaging Robots Market by Gripper Type (Claw, Clamp, Vacuum and Others), Application (Picking & Placing, Packing and Palletizing) and End User (Food & Beverage, Pharmaceutical, Logistics, Consumer Products, Logistics and Others) – Global Opportunity Analysis and Industry Forecast, 2017–2023." Allied Market Research. May 2017. Accessed April 05, 2019. https://www.alliedmarketresearch.com/packaging-robots-market.
7 Loomba, Smriti. "Packaging Robots Market by Gripper Type (Claw, Clamp, Vacuum and Others), Application (Picking & Placing, Packing and Palletizing) and End User (Food & Beverage, Pharmaceutical, Logistics, Consumer Products, Logistics and Others) – Global Opportunity Analysis and Industry Forecast, 2017–2023." Allied Market Research. May 2017. Accessed April 05, 2019. https://www.alliedmarketresearch.com/packaging-robots-market.

Industries Limited, and Yaskawa America Inc., among others.[8] The NRP R&D team's recent analysis of the patents held by the majority of dominant players revealed that the existing packaging robots lacked the ability to detect and distinguish among objects and were used only for specific activities. A specific end-effector could only grip a predetermined object. Hence, it was apparent that the next generation of end-effectors integrated with developed technologies such as three-dimensional (3D) vision and tactile sensing could enter the packaging robot market without much barrier.

Surgical robots industry

Surgical robots used by surgeons generally consisted of miniaturized surgical instruments which were mounted on robotic arms, enabling precise surgeries. The global surgical robotics market was valued at US$56,294.9 million in 2017 and was expected to reach US$98,737.0 million by 2024 at a CAGR of 8.5 percent during the forecast period.[9] The key factors driving the surgical robotics market size were the increasing need for automation in the healthcare industry and the shifting trend towards advanced robotic surgeries. However, the high cost associated with surgical robotic surgeries and robotic systems would have hampered the medical robots market.[10]

North America dominated the global surgical robotics market in 2017 and was expected to retain its dominance throughout the forecast period. This was attributed to the well-established healthcare infrastructure and the increase in adoption of surgical robotic systems across various healthcare settings.[11]

---

8 MarketsandMarkets. "Industrial Robotics Market worth 71.72 Billion USD by 2023." News release, July 2017. MarketsandMarkets. Accessed April 14, 2019. https://www.marketsandmarkets.com/PressReleases/industrial-robotics.asp.

9 Loomba, Smriti. "Packaging Robots Market by Gripper Type (Claw, Clamp, Vacuum and Others), Application (Picking & Placing, Packing and Palletizing) and End User (Food & Beverage, Pharmaceutical, Logistics, Consumer Products, Logistics and Others) – Global Opportunity Analysis and Industry Forecast, 2017–2023." Allied Market Research. May 2017. Accessed April 05, 2019. https://www.alliedmarketresearch.com/packaging-robots-market.

10 Sajeev, Surak, and Garima Chandra. "Surgical Robotics Market by Component (Systems, Accessories and Services), by Surgery Type (Gynecology Surgery, Urology Surgery, Neurosurgery, Orthopedic Surgery, General Surgery and Other Surgeries): Global Opportunity Analysis and Industry Forecast, 2017 – 2024." Allied Market Research. April 2018. Accessed April 05, 2019. https://www.alliedmarketresearch.com/surgical-robotics-market.

11 Loomba, Smriti. "Packaging Robots Market by Gripper Type (Claw, Clamp, Vacuum and Others), Application (Picking & Placing, Packing and Palletizing) and End User (Food & Beverage, Pharmaceutical, Logistics, Consumer Products, Logistics and Others) – Global Opportunity Analysis and Industry Forecast, 2017–2023." Allied Market Research. May 2017. Accessed April 05, 2019. https://www.alliedmarketresearch.com/packaging-robots-market.

The Allied Market Research report had identified the key players operating in the global 3D medical imaging services market: Smith & Nephew Plc. (Blue Belt Technologies, Inc.), Auris Surgical Robotics, Inc. (Hansen Medical Inc.), Intuitive Surgical, Inc., KUKA AG, Stryker Corporation (MAKO Surgical Corp.), Mazor Robotics, Renishaw plc, Medtronic plc, THINK Surgical Inc., and Zimmer Biomet Holdings Inc.[12] Other players operating in the value chain were Transenterix, Verb Surgical, Titan Medical, Microbot Medical, Accuray and Medrobotics. A major market player, Intuitive Surgical, maker of the da Vinci Surgical System, had trained over 44,000 surgeons, across 66 countries, to use its systems.[13] However, these systems lacked tactile sensing and the ability to handle non-standardized objects.

It was apparent that there was a lack of robotic end-effectors that could handle assorted objects with tactile sense, thus providing a good opportunity for development and innovation in this area of the industry.

Developing a commercialization strategy

Back in May 2018, the NRP R&D team collaborated with Professor Sarah Cheah of the National University of Singapore (NUS) Business School to develop a commercialization strategy for a group of robotics R&D projects. To develop the strategy, the commercialization team led by Cheah started with literature review to identify related robotics ecosystem and its stakeholders that the team could interview to validate the hypotheses about the market demand and might have a potential interest in commercializing any of the R&D projects.

To optimize the interview opportunities with the stakeholders, three analysis frameworks were adopted, with each addressing distinct aspects of the R&D projects: (a) customer discovery process to determine the value proposition of project application,[14] (b) commercial potential assessment framework to assess the commercial potential of the underlying IP of the project,[15] and (c) quality function

---

12 Loomba, Smriti. "Packaging Robots Market by Gripper Type (Claw, Clamp, Vacuum and Others), Application (Picking & Placing, Packing and Palletizing) and End User (Food & Beverage, Pharmaceutical, Logistics, Consumer Products, Logistics and Others) – Global Opportunity Analysis and Industry Forecast, 2017–2023." Allied Market Research. May 2017. Accessed April 05, 2019. https://www.alliedmarketresearch.com/packaging-robots-market.

13 Intuitive, accessed on April 14, 2019. https://www.intuitive.com/

14 Blank, Steve. "Steve Blank Customer Discovery." Steve Blank. 2009. Accessed April 10, 2019. https://steveblank.com/tag/customer-discovery/.

15 Bandarian, Reza. "Measuring Commercial Potential of a New Technology at the Early Stage of Development with Fuzzy Logic." *Journal of Technology Management and Innovation*, 2007. 2007. Accessed April 11, 2019. https://www.researchgate.net/publication/26496753_Measuring_Commercial_Potential_of_a_New_Technology_at_the_Early_Stage_of_Development_with_Fuzzy_Logic.

deployment (QFD) to translate identified customer needs into quantitative technical specifications for the development of new products that embody the underlying project IP.[16]

Stakeholder analysis

Before developing a commercialization strategy, it would be important to identify the relevant stakeholders in the robotics ecosystem. Reaching out to them to hear their views and perceptions about the industry would help validate one's assumptions about the pain points of the target customers, understand possible opportunities and threats to one's model of growth trajectory, as well as identify potential customers, partners, suppliers or competitors to one's roadmap of product and solution offerings. Some of the stakeholders who were willing to be interviewed could help to validate the hypothesized value propositions of the technology, suggest improvements or changes to the value propositions of the technology and gain new insights from industry experts on market forecast and technological trends.

The stakeholders that might have had potential interest in commercializing the end-effector project were identified through market reports by consulting firms (e.g. Frost & Sullivan and Allied Market Research), research or practitioner journals (e.g. European Scientific Journal and Robotics), patent databases (e.g. PatSnap) and conferences and exhibitions by associations (e.g. Singapore Industrial and Automation Association), and referrals through technology and industry experts.

From literature review, conference visits and referrals, the commercialization team identified more than 60 stakeholders in the robotics ecosystem and its larger environment. These stakeholders could be categorized into three groups. The first group comprised the R&D performers including the public research institutes, universities and private industrial research laboratories. The second group was made up of system integrators including vendors that provided product and custom solution offerings in the related application domains. The third group consisted of adopters involving private and public organizations that were potential candidates for implementing products/solutions embodying the related applications. Of the population of 64 stakeholders, 22 organizations/individuals were selected by reason of close proximity in geographical distance, research domain and commercial applications. The sampling frame of 22 stakeholders was expected to provide a fair representation of key markets (environment and healthcare) and stakeholder types (system integrator, adopter and R&D performer).

---

16 Akao, Yoji, Bob King, and Glenn H. Mazur. Quality function deployment: integrating customer requirements into product design. Vol. 21. Cambridge, MA: Productivity press, 1990.

Out of the 22 stakeholders contacted between June and July 2018, 14 stakeholders responded positively to the team's request for in-depth interviews. Analysis of the respondent profile showed a fair representation of the three stakeholder categories – 29 percent R&D performers, 43 percent system integrators and 29 percent adopters – with participation in key markets. Prior to the interviews, the commercialization team prepared an information sheet on each interviewee company to learn more about its products and operations to increase the effectiveness of the interview session. The key stakeholder representatives that were sought for the interviews were the chief executives of top market players in the robotics industry, product managers, technology or innovation managers and key opinion leaders.

Some of the selected stakeholders were system integrators which could be potential IP licensees or R&D partners. They could offer pertinent advice on the commercial viability and technological feasibility of the project applications from their extensive experience in integrating robots or automation solutions. The R&D performers could provide insights on the technology from a researcher's point of view. They would be able to inform the team about the difficulties that they had faced while developing end-effectors. If they had prior spin-off experience, they would be a useful resource for understanding the startup challenges in the robotics field. The adopters were selected because they could enlighten the team about the problems faced by the end users of existing end-effectors, the price-performance situation of the end-effectors and possible use cases of high utility value to the end users.

The views from a range of stakeholder types gathered through interviews would provide important input about (a) the value proposition examined in the customer discovery process, (b) customer requirements and technical specifications required in the QFD, and (c) commercial potential assessment. All these would be considered in the formulation of a commercialization strategy.

Customer discovery process

The customer discovery process was a market research technique seeking to understand customer needs and using a hypothesis-driven approach to determine the value proposition of a new product application. In conceiving new product application, one would have certain assumptions about customer problems and the desired solution. However, these assumptions are hypotheses that should be validated. By turning hypotheses into a prototype, known as a minimum viable product (MVP), the process encouraged putting that prototype or MVP in the hands of a stakeholder or potential customer to gather feedback. Previously, companies operated in 'stealth mode', revealing prototypes of their product to customers only during 'beta' tests.[17] The problem with this method was that feedback was obtained only after the complete product was formed and launched. Very often, it was found that customers did not need or want most of the product features. The frequent interaction with stakeholders in the customer discovery process allowed for iterative feedback loops which in turn yielded better results compared to the 'stealth mode' of operation.

To determine the value proposition, the commercialization team prepared MVP in the form of PowerPoint presentation decks that highlighted the pain points, value proposition, use cases with the proposed solution applications, and commercialization pathways (IP licensing, R&D collaboration, spin-off). The pain points presented in the deck highlighted that end-effectors were mainly developed for industrial use and were unable to handle fragile and assorted items.[18] The value propositions were therefore lightweight and soft end-effectors that combined tactile sensing, computer vision and machine learning that had high flexibility, and were able to pick up items of varying sizes, weights and shapes.[19] The team proposed use cases of this technology in cleaning robots and surgical robots. These MVP decks were then presented to various stakeholders as discussion points for the interviews.

The MVP decks were created to allow the presenters to interact with the stakeholders, who could share their views of the severity and significance of the pain points, visualize the proposed solution applications and articulate their feedback on their relevance and attractiveness in price-performance ratios. Semi-structured questionnaires that were customized for each type of stakeholders, were designed and administered to supplement the MVP decks to capture quantifiable responses from the stakeholders. The flow of the questionnaire allowed for the stakeholders to express their views on how robotics and computer vision would develop, before moving on to discuss the challenges faced with existing end-effectors and then voicing their opinion on the MVP. The questions also aimed to find out the current market prices of end-effectors in various industries and how they would price the MVP. They were also asked to rate the MVP on the following aspects: feasibility, industry adoption and adoption by the stakeholders themselves. Follow-up questions were asked based on the ratings to identify and prioritize customer requirements. The interview ended with the stakeholders discussing their preferred mode of commercialization for the product.

17 Blank, Steve. "Why the Lean Start-Up Changes Everything." Harvard Business Review. February 09, 2018. Accessed April 14, 2019. https://hbr.org/2013/05/why-the-lean-start-up-changes-everything.

18 Tai, Kevin, Abdul-Rahman El-Sayed, Mohammadali Shahriari, Mohammad Biglarbegian, and Shohel Mahmud. "State Of The Art Robotic Grippers And Applications". *Robotics*, 2016, 5 (2): 11. doi:10.3390/robotics5020011.

19 Frost & Sullivan. "Industrial Robotics – Decoding the Robotics Impact on Manufacturing". Report. 2016. Accessed April 14, 2019.

During an interview of hospital management staff, one manager did not just validate the pain points but also informed the team about other pain points that the commercialization team was not aware of, such as high costs and lack of tactile sensing, especially in surgical robots such as da Vinci systems:

> There is capital cost, which is high, which is US$4M for purchasing (a da Vinci system), then there are annual running costs for quarter million, just for preventive maintenance. That is just the machine and then you have the consumables. Every time you use it, you use instruments, they have built-in shelf life, because they want to make money. Every time we do a surgery, we have to change the instruments, and the costs range from US$500 to US$800 to US$1000 per patient and use. Different instruments have different costs, it's not cheap.

Another manager from the same hospital echoed the pain point by highlighting, "da Vinci doesn't have tactile sensing. Maybe next generation will have. With tactile sensation, it can tell where you are, so if it hits a bone, you will know."

The interviews suggested that the gripper technology integrated with computer vision could be useful in the surgical robot industry and the 'pick and place' industry. One research performer even suggested that the technology could be used in homes, "In the home context, everything of daily life. Maybe loading a refrigerator, loading and unloading a washing machine and dryer."

Quality function deployment

Quality function deployment (QFD) was an approach developed by Yoji Akao in Japan since 1966 to help transform the voice of the customer into engineering characteristics for a product. It was a method that would take qualitative customer needs into consideration and transforming these demands into quantitative technical specifications for product development.

The QFD methodology was used to communicate customer needs to multiple business operations throughout an organization including design, quality, manufacturing, production, marketing and sales. This effective communication of the voice of the customer allowed the entire organization to work together and produce products with high levels of customer perceived value.[20] QFD reduced the likelihood of late design changes by focusing on product features and improvements based on customer requirements. This prevented time and resources from being wasted on the development of non-value added features. It provided a structured method and various tools for recording decisions made and lessons learned during the product development process.

20 "Quality Function Deployment (QFD)." Quality-One. Accessed April 14, 2019. https://quality-one.com/qfd/#Why.

The primary functions of QFD included product development, quality management, and customer needs analysis.

In 1986, Chrysler Motor Corporation, a US-based automobile manufacturer, successfully implemented QFD in the launch of LH platform for mid-size cars. Compared to the previous product design cycles of 54 to 62 months, QFD reduced the cycle time to approximately 36 months. Only 740 people were required in the QFD program, a significant improvement over a staff strength of 1600 people in the previous environment.[21] By focusing on customer requirements instead of cost only, Chrysler made innovative design changes that gained acceptance in the marketplace.

One key method used in QFD is the House of Quality. It was a planning matrix that would classify customer requirements and rank them in order of importance. Subsequently, these requirements were matched to relevant design characteristics by ranking of correlation. To build the House of Quality, it would be important to first understand the needs of the customer, followed by the importance of these needs to the customer. These requirements were then translated into design specifi- cations and changes in each specification would affect the perception of the customer.

The first step of a QFD process was 'customer needs analysis',[22] which the com- mercialization team accomplished through the stakeholder interviews. A 'House of Quality' was then built to match customer needs with the concerned design specifications.

Several important pain points were highlighted by the stakeholders during the interviews. One revolved around the price of current end-effectors. All the stake- holders wanted cheaper yet highly functioning end-effectors. In an interview with a stakeholder operating in a hospital, it was found that tactile sensing was a feature in high demand in surgical robots. The same stakeholder felt that "In hospitals, safety is very important if the robots are interacting with humans."

A system integrator, on the other hand, felt that end-effectors should be com- pact, safe and soft, "The more sensors you combine, the heavier it will get. We will need soft grippers for good human interface or collaboration". Other system inte- grators wanted end-effectors to have a long useful life, have the ability to handle high loads and have active and passive compliance. They also wanted them to be efficient and have faster pick-up and delivery.

---

21 Chen, Chi-Ming, and Victor Susanto. "Quality Function Deployment (QFD)." Quality Function Deployment (QFD). Accessed April 14, 2019. https://vardeman.public.iastate.edu/IE361/s00mini/chen.htm.

22 Callegaro, Aline Marian, Carla Schwengber ten Caten, Raffaela Leane Zenni Tanure, Amanda Sória Buss, Márcia Elisa Soares Echeveste, and Carlos Fernando Jung. "Managing requirements for the development of a novel elbow rehabilitation device." *Technological Forecasting and Social Change* 113 (2016): 404–411.

The customer requirements articulated by the stakeholders during the interviews were then translated into ten corresponding quality characteristics that would have to be considered in the development of new products embodying the end-effector technology. The interviews were very helpful in establishing a link between certain customer needs and their corresponding design characteristics. Some of the interview responses included: "AI, computer vision and tactile sensing are important in surgical robots, making them more efficient"

In this manner, all the quality characteristics were identified: (a) size, (b) cost, (c) safety, (d) performance, (e) speed, (f) useful life, (g) sensors, (h) softness, (i) hardware and (j) AI, machine learning and other software. The interviews enabled the team to establish the nature of correlation between 'customer needs' and 'design specification'. For example, it was found that there was a strong correlation between customer need 'safety' and design characteristic 'sensors', and a weak relationship between 'long useful life' and 'speed': "If the robot moves fast, or has high speed, it can be expected the use life will be low".

Commercial potential

The commercial potential was the opportunity of commercializing a candidate technology or IP. To satisfy market needs, every new technology had to find its fit in a continuously changing and unpredictable business environment. Assessment of the commercial potential of a technology was a critical element for formulating successful commercialization strategies.

The commercialization team used the commercial potential assessment framework to assess the commercial potential of the underlying IP of the gripper technology integrated with computer vision project. The framework comprised a set of three dimensions (technology, commercialization and market) with eight indicators (e.g. competitive advantage of technology, licensing/ collaboration potential, commercial readiness, and market growth potential).

A four-point scoring system was used to rate the various aspects of the underlying technology, with one being the least fitting and four being the best fitting. The higher the level attained, the higher the score achieved for the indicator.

Technology

The technology dimension measured the technological aspect of the underlying technology. The indicators in this dimension measured its technological competitiveness in the industry. This competitiveness was measured in terms of the quality of the technology developed. The higher the quality of the technology, the greater the competitive advantage.[23] The three indicators in this dimension were (a) competitive advantage of technology, (b) IP strength and (c) technology relevance and readiness.

The proposed robotics end-effectors stood out from the existing products in the market in terms of performance and cost benchmarking. The technology readiness level (TRL) was rated at TRL 3, where there was proof of concept with full scientific feasibility demonstrated in laboratory. Recommendations were made by the stakeholders during interviews that "It should be able to carry heavy loads at good speeds."

The CEO of a certain system integrator company proposed that there should be good integration between software and hardware: "There should be active and passive compliance. The software and the hardware have to work together efficiently."

Commercialization

The commercialization dimension measured the commercial readiness of the underlying technology with five indicators: engagement with stakeholders, licensing/collaboration potential, product demand, commercial readiness, and market growth potential. These indicators measured the demand for the technology in the industry. The higher the demand, the greater was the commercial potential of the technology.

The value proposition was validated by the stakeholder interviews, while the MVP received a great deal of positive feedback, especially from the stakeholders in the healthcare industry. One commented, "There is a need for artificial intelligence, tactile sensing and computer vision in surgical robots. They will help us see in regions we can't reach ... If it is not very expensive, it has a lot of market potential." Another opined, "If it can pick any item, it would be useful to pick and sterilize assorted surgical instruments with ease, thus helping nurses and saving time."

Although there was a clear demand for such technology in the market, the proposed application was not ready to be commercialized as a product as it required more R&D.

Market

The market dimension measured the market sizing for the technology. It gave a fair representation of the target market and helped to assess if it was large and

---

23 Zorrilla, Dolores Margarita Navarrete, Tirso Javier Hernández Gracia, Del Rosario García Velazquez, Jose Francisco Hernandez Gracia, Jose Gustavo Ibarra Duran, and Juan Alberto Carranza Sevilla. "Relevance of Technological Innovation in the Business Competitiveness of Medium Enterprises in Hidalgo State." *European Scientific Journal* 10, no. 16 (2014). Accessed April 10, 2019. https://eujournal.org/index.php/esj/article/view/3532/3304.

scalable for commercialization to be viable. In order to gauge the commercial via-bility and potential of a project, it was critical to consider market sizing to judge the revenue generating potential of the technology. The indicator in this dimen-sion was market growth potential, which was an indicator to estimate market growth based on CAGR.

The project expected a rapid growth forecast with a CAGR of at least ten per-cent. The stakeholder interviews revealed that the target market for end-effectors with tactile sensing, machine learning and computer vision was the healthcare in-dustry since the need for such end-effectors, especially in surgical robots, was high. An adopter of surgical robots asserted, "Surgical robots need tactile sensing and computer vision. Right now, there are no such products in the market".

Based on the stakeholder interview responses, the gripper technology inte-grated with computer vision project was given a total score which reflected the overall commercial potential of the technology. The project was given a rating of 79 percent in the commercialization dimension, 100 percent in the market and 42 percent in the technology dimension.

Commercialization pathways

From the analysis of stakeholder interview responses supplemented by literature re-view, the commercialization pathways under consideration were (a) IP licensing to existing companies, (b) R&D collaboration and (c) spin-off.

IP licensing

IP licensing referred to an agreement where one organization ("licensor") would grant another organization ("licensee") the right to commercialize its IP in desig-nated geographical regions (where the IP had been filed for and/or granted protec-tion) for a stipulated tenure in exchange for upfront fee and recurring royalty payments typically as a percentage of the licensee's sales of its products that em-bodied the licensed IP.

Before licensing out any IP, the licensor had to consider several factors. Among them was the "exclusiveness" of the IP arrangement that had important implica-tions. Public sector research institutes would generally grant companies the right to commercialize their IP on a non-exclusive basis, with the view that the public-funded IP should benefit as many companies as possible. This principle of non-exclusiveness would also protect the licensor from licensees who were not committed to genuine commercialization effort. However, companies would prefer an exclusive licensing arrangement since they saw the IP as an important asset that could serve as an entry barrier to their industry and give them a competitive advantage. Without exclusive licensing, companies would be less willing to invest much resources and time to develop the IP and integrate it into their existing or new product or service offerings. In the event that a particular company might be the only one or one of the few organizations willing or capable of commercializing certain IP for some unique reasons, the licensor might be more willing to grant the right to commercialize their IP on an exclusive basis.[24]

In 2003, Pieris Pharmaceuticals, Inc. (PIRS) and the Technical University of Munich (TUM), Germany, had entered into a Research and License Agreement wherein TUM had exclusively licensed its Anticalin protein-related IP to PIRS.[25] However, in 2015, PIRS initiated arbitration hearings to address issues regarding the calculation of payments due from PIRS to TUM. These payments due were the result of PIRS's out-licensing revenues attributable to IP covered by the Research and Licensing Agreement from 2004 to 2012. TUM had asserted that the out-licensing fee due from Pieris was €2,529,400[26] plus interest, while PIRS had calculated the out-licensing fee owed as approximately €0.4 million. The German Institute of Arbitration ruled that the amount of out-licensing fees due for the disputed period was €859,854 and that TUM must reimburse Pieris €110,000 for fees incurred and had dismissed TUM's claim for reimbursement of its costs. After factoring in account interest payable on the out-licensing fee of €167,234, along with certain credits and the award of PIRS' fees, the total amount payable by PIRS to TUM was approximately €917,088.[27]

When choosing between an established company and a startup to license the IP to, the licensor had to consider their ability and motivation to commercialize. Compared with startups, companies would have had more resources at their disposal to commercialize the IP. On the other hand, companies might not be as motivated as startups to exploit the licensed IP since the former would also have existing product and service offerings that could compete for limited internal resources.

A majority of the stakeholders interviewed ranging from system integrators to adopters preferred licensing. However, an adopter from the healthcare industry indicated that it would choose to license only if it was the most mutually beneficial

---

24 "Guidelines for Technology Transfer." AUTM. 2007. Accessed April 17, 2019. https://autm.net/about-tech-transfer/principles-and-guidelines/nine-points-to-consider-when-licensing-university.
25 "Intellectual Property." Pieris Pharmaceuticals. Accessed April 18, 2019. https://www.pieris.com/anticalin-technology/intellectual-property.
26 € = EUR = Euro; €1~ US$ 1.13 as of April 12, 2019.
27 Bautz, David. "PIRS: Attains Favorable Ruling in Arbitration with TUM; Continued Positive Developments from Collaborations." Yahoo! Finance. December 02, 2015. Accessed April 18, 2019. https://finance.yahoo.com/news/pirs-attains-favorable-ruling-arbitration-170500251.html.

option and if the technology would require licensing. Otherwise, they would prefer R&D collaboration or purchasing the IP.

R&D collaboration

R&D collaboration referred to an agreement between participating organizations that aimed to perform R&D together. In such a mode of cooperation, the collaborators typically retained their rights to their own existing IP (background IP). The ownership of new IP that would be generated as a result of the collaboration (also known as the foreground IP) was subject to negotiation between the parties involved, depending on the nature and amount of investment each party committed to the collaboration.

Collaborations allowed researchers with different backgrounds to interact and solve a specific problem and might even help researchers with their own research. A system integrator specializing in the 'pick and place' industry observed, "R&D alliance is something you will need in many cases. When you stop investing in R&D, you will be dying. So, we are doing internally, and in collaboration with universities and technology institutes."

In 2017, the EXPLORER consortium from UC Davis, USA, had partnered with United Imaging Healthcare America, a North American subsidiary of Shanghai United Imaging Healthcare and SensL Technologies of Cork, Ireland, to build a total-body positron emission tomography (PET) scanner.[28] In May 2018, the collaboration proved successful when the consortium unveiled the world's first total-body PET scanner and in November 2018,[29] the first human images from the scanner were unveiled at the IEEE MIC 2018 Total-Body PET workshop, Australia.[30]

As in every relationship, collaboration could be tricky as disagreements could arise between the parties on matters ranging from the priority to be accorded to research projects to liabilities to the costs incurred or claims to the results obtained. Sometimes collaborations could take much longer than anticipated. In a research collaboration, there could be problems relating to assigning credit to the participants, resulting in conflict.[31]

---

28 "SensL Announces United Imaging Healthcare and UC-Davis Collaboration for SiPM Based System." SensL. January 17, 2017. Accessed April 18, 2019. https://sensl.com/sensl-united-imaging/.

29 Workshop conducted at 2018 IEEE Nuclear Science Symposium and Medical Imaging Conference, Sydney, Australia.

30 "Human Images From World's 1st Total-Body Scanner Unveiled." EXPLORER. November 2018. Accessed April 18, 2019. https://explorer.ucdavis.edu/news.

31 Wray, K. B. "Scientific Authorship in the Age of Collaborative Research." *Studies in History and Philosophy of Science* Part A37, no. 3 (September 2004): 504–15. Accessed April 13, 2019. doi: https://doi.org/10.1016/j.shpsa.2005.07.011.

The interviews revealed that if a project was in its initial stages with a relatively low TRL, certain adopters and system integrators would prefer R&D collaboration. A few system integrators and researchers also expressed interest in this mode of commercialization.

Spin-off

Spin-off referred to the creation of a new legal entity to design and produce its products. Spin-off companies were new companies that would commercialize a research result from the parent organization through a license agreement.[32] The spin-off would enable the research team to operate independently and continue its work in the original IP.

There was a general consensus among the stakeholders that it was very important for a spin-off to maintain a strong link with its parent research institute as well as other research institutions to keep abreast with technological advancements. A system integrator remarked:

> Many of the companies that are now in the market, are losing. They are losing because they don't have direct link with universities or schools. So, they are not able to find the right people for their applications, their production lines, their design, testing or something like that. Being a spin-off, it allows you to maintain the link to know the principal investor, to the students there, to pick excellence in each and every sector.

The Taiwan Semiconductor Manufacturing Company (TSMC) was a successful spinoff from the Industrial Technology Research Institute (ITRI), Taiwan. It was founded in 1987 by Morris Chang, the then chairman and president of ITRI. Over the years, TSMC became one of the world's most profitable chip makers supplying chips to Apple Inc.[33] In 2017, TSMC's market capitalization had hit US$168.4 billion, surpassing semiconductor giant Intel's US$165.7 billion.[34]

The stakeholders also highlighted the problems a spin-off could face such as funding and lack of resources. While working in a university or technological institute with adequate research grants, funding might not be an issue. However, after

---

32 Rast, Sadegh, Navid Khabiri, and Aslan Amat Senin. "Evaluation Framework for Assessing University-Industry Collaborative Research and Technological Initiative." *Procedia – Social and Behavioral Sciences*, 2012, 410–16. Accessed April 12, 2019. doi: 10.1016/j.sbspro.2012.03.208.

33 "TSMC Kicks Off A6 Processor Trial Production with Apple." Taiwan Economic News. 2011. Accessed April 18, 2019. https://web.archive.org/web/20110927000244/http://cens.com/cens/html/en/news/news_inner_37282.html.

34 Culpan, Tim. "Chipzilla Got Toppled." Bloomberg Opinion. March 22, 2017. Accessed April 18, 2019. https://www.bloomberg.com/opinion/articles/2017-03-22/chipzilla-intel-toppled-by-taiwan-s-supplier-to-the-stars.

the spin-off, funding, finding facilities, managing resources and hiring the right people would become a problem as the spin-off had to build its resources, customers and supply chain from scratch.

Empire Robotics, Inc. was founded in 2012 to commercialize a gripper technology VERSABALL that was developed at Cornell University and the University of Chicago, USA.[35] The spinoff had even won US$10,000 at the LES Foundation 2013 International Graduate Student Business Plan Competition awarded by Licensing Executives Society, USA.[36] The spinoff had won prize money in various other business plan competitions, raised private investment funds, exhibited at over twenty industry trade shows and generated US$500,000 in revenue from product sales.[37] However, the company was not able to commercialize its technology adequately. As a result, the spinoff shut down its operations in 2016.

A system integrator in the 'pick and place' industry cautioned:

> Talking about spin-off, I think you should keep a strong link between research centers and institutes. This is something you will have, and your competitor will not have, and this is a plus for you. To have a company, a spin-off, to realize the technology transfer is important to not let the research die in the collaboration... There are challenges to spin-off. First of all, the finance is the problem. When you are inside the university, or the school or the technology institute, you don't care about finance or the funds, but when you are a spin-off, you are a private company, so you would face problems, in hiring people, in finding facilities, that is costly in our world.

At the end of the commercialization strategy development project, the commercialization team presented the findings of the stakeholder interviews, customer discovery, QFD and commercial potential assessment, as well as recommendations to the NRP R&D team.

Moving forward

As the team went through results and suggestions from the commercialization team, they pondered over the next steps with the commercialization of the gripper technology with computer vision project. Should the technology be licensed in its

---

35 "About Us – Empire Robotics." Empire Robotics. Accessed April 18, 2019. https://www.empirero botics.com/about/.

36 Licensing Executives Society. "Cornell University Spinout Empire Robotics Wins LES Foundation Competiton." News release, May 16, 2013. LES. Accessed April 18, 2019. https://www.lesusacanada.org/news/266350/Cornell-University-Spinout-Empire-Robotics-Wins-LES-Foundation-Competiton.htm.

37 "Lessons Learned: Empire Robotics Explains Failed Attempt to Commercialize Soft Robotics Technology." 3DPrint.com | The Voice of 3D Printing / Additive Manufacturing. January 19, 2017. Accessed April 18, 2019. https://3dprint.com/162151/versaball-lessons-learned/.

current state to existing companies? Or should it be developed further in collaboration with other partners? Or should it support spin-off from the parent research organization and be its own entity?

Learning objectives

This case aims to illustrate the following:
- Importance of the intervention phase of SFM to develop R&D plans and commercialization pathways to create and capture future value.
- Importance of identifying and analyzing stakeholders who provide important input about the value proposition of new product applications.
- Relevance of customer discovery process in identifying potential customers, ascertaining product-market fit, as well as developing commercially viable business models.
- Utilization of multi-dimensional framework to assess the commercial potential of new product applications.
- Importance of quality function deployment process to capture and map customer requirements into new product functionalities.

8 Conclusion

This book sets out to highlight the importance of conducting foresight in organizations to manage the complexity and ambiguity of the future operating environment. Through real-life cases, it highlights a range of foresight methods available to organizations to formulate and implement strategic plans based on findings from the various phases of the systemic foresight methodology (SFM). By fleshing out their strengths and limitations, it illuminates the complementarity of the various foresight methods in each phase to achieve organizational goals.

In this chapter, several salient takeaways from the publication are emphasized.

The takeaways

Broad categorization of technologies and deep dive

In the intelligence phase of SFM, the information sources typically comprise expert opinions, trade reports and academic journals. However, when dealing with emerging technologies, the field of research is likely to be nascent and the classifications broad. While the general categories used by the various sources might be useful for understanding the prevailing adoption rate at industry levels, they would be too broad for searching and identifying possible applications for solving industry problems. As highlighted in Chapter 3, the broad categorization makes it challenging to perform horizon scanning. To address the challenge, organizations should dive deep into the topic to identify the relevant stream of literature, as well as conduct a search on a range of other related technologies. It is critical to be specific in the search process and delve into the scientific specialization of the technology applications.

Inconsistent nomenclature and linkage creation

The broad categorization of emerging technologies is exacerbated by the lack of standardization in taxonomy across the various communities ranging from market analysts to research performers. The inconsistency in nomenclature from discipline to discipline makes it difficult to understand the constituent elements of the target technology so that appropriate keywords could be identified and input for meaningful patent search results. As noted by Ooi in Chapter 4, "patent configuration is very different from human understanding . . . they go by product categories, number sequence, the taxonomy is very different from human understanding. It is not easy to find. It needs a lot of effort to understand." To tackle this challenge, organizations should complement patent analysis with review of scientific literature to

https://doi.org/10.1515/9783110672916-008

create linkages between parcels of information gleaned throughout the patent search process. To have clarity on the current and future states of technology, it is important to examine the list of patents extracted from the search, discard the irrelevant ones, annotate the relevant ones for linkages, identify new search keys from the patent contents and refine search terms. After repeating multiple iterations of the search, organizations are then well positioned to locate a certain technology sub-category that can serve as a good lead into further patent searches.

Applicability of contexts and opportunity identification

Apart from the fragmented literature, organizations can encounter the challenge of searching and identifying solutions that can address the specific needs of their target geographical market. What had worked well in other countries might not work well in the target market due to its distinct characteristics. As illustrated in Chapter 3, the ultra-high density of land-scarce countries such as Singapore had made it impossible to simply import robotics solutions from other countries. Service robots that were designed for the wide aisles of overseas hospitals, for example, were found to be too bulky for the narrow aisles of Singapore hospitals. It is apparent that the space constraints in Singapore would require different types of service robots to meet its requirements. The ultra-high population density of the country would make existing robotic solutions of other countries irrelevant. On the other hand, this limitation presents a rare opportunity for Singapore to develop the next-generation of robots to address its unique requirements. As other cities continue to grow in density from intensive urbanization, they will eventually be confronted with the same issue of ultra-high population density as Singapore and are therefore likely to find Singapore's solutions relevant in the future.

Tracking technology development in non-English speaking countries

In the recent decade, we have witnessed a significant growth in patent volume and impact from economic powerhouses, particularly China, Japan and South Korea. However, their patents are difficult to retrieve as they have been filed in local languages with their countries' intellectual property office systems. Organizations operating in English speaking countries will find it hard to identify and track technology development in non-English speaking countries. The language barrier is a big obstacle when it comes to searching for patents in such countries, as depicted in Chapter 4. To overcome this obstacle, it is essential to gather technology intelligence from other sources such as attending international exhibitions and conferences to gain access to other companies' technological advances that have not been codified into English publications or filed as patents in English language.

Static roadmapping in a dynamic environment

Roadmapping is an important strategic foresight method for identifying emergent market and technology trends, and drawing up plans for systematic resource allocation to capture the opportunities presented in the long-term future. However, the volatility and uncertainty of the external environment might render the roadmap irrelevant or obsolete in the short- to mid-term future, as described in Chapter 6. Some policymakers may respond to this challenge by shortening their planning cycles to generate a more dynamic roadmap to adapt to external turbulences. Others see the value of long-term plans and refer to them retroactively as a guide for future development and a baseline for tracking social and technological realization.

New evidence base for foresight with technological advances

The growing complexity and diversity of modern cities have made policy formulation and strategic planning more difficult. With advances in computing and telecommunication technologies, data volume continues to grow from multiple sources ranging from social media to sensors and devices. Computer-aided systems will therefore play a greater role in mining data for weak signals and monitoring trends. As computer-aided systems are able to learn and build up knowledge over time, they can complement the established foresight methods to provide new evidence base for future planning. This will allow the shift of domain expertise from the early phases of corporate foresight process (intelligence and imagination) to the later stages (integration, interpretation and intervention), thereby mitigating human bias.

In concluding, we hope that this book will encourage organizations to adopt a holistic and systemic foresight approach to chart their future growth trajectory.

References

Akao, Y. and Mazur, G. H. (2003). The leading edge in QFD: past, present and future. *International Journal of Quality & Reliability Management*, *20*(1), 20–35.

Aydogdu, A., Burmaoglu, S., Saritas, O. and Cakir, S. (2017). A nanotechnology roadmapping study for the Turkish defense industry, *Foresight*, *19*(4), 354–375.

Badger, D., Nursten, J., Williams, P. and Woodward, M. (2000). Should all literature reviews be systematic?. *Evaluation & Research in Education*, *14*(3–4), 220–230.

Bakhtin, P. and Saritas, O. (2016). Tech mining for emerging STI trends through dynamic term clustering and semantic analysis: The case of Photonics, Anticipating Future Innovation Pathways through Large Data Analytics, eds. T.U. Daim, D. Chiavetta, A.L. Porter, and O. Saritas, Springer Verlag, Berlin, 341–360.

Bakhtin, P., Saritas, O., Chulok, A., Kuzminov, I. and Timofeev, A. (2017). Trend monitoring for linking science and strategy, *Scientometrics*, *111*(3), 2059–2075.

Bezold, C. (2010). Lessons from using scenarios for strategic foresight. *Technological forecasting and social change*, *77*(9), 1513–1518.

Blank, S. (2013). Why the lean start-up changes everything. *Harvard business review*, *91*(5), 63–72.

Burmaoglu, S. and Saritas, O. (2017). Changing characteristics of warfare and the future of military R&D, *Technological Forecasting and Social Change*, *116*, 151–161.

Burmaoglu, S. and Saritas, O. (2019). An evolutionary analysis of innovation policy: Is there a paradigm shift? Scientometrics, https://doi.org/10.1007/s11192-019-03014-1.

Burmaoglu, S. and Saritas, O. (2020). Science, Technology and Innovation policy development in a network society: Transition to a distributed, decentralized and uncensored perspective with IdeaChain, *Foresight*, forthcoming.

Burmaoglu, S., Saritas, O., Kidak, L. and Camuz, I. (2017). Evolution of connected health: a network perspective, *Scientometrics*, *112*(3), 1419–1438.

Çetindamar, D., Phaal, R. and Probert, D. (2016). Technology management: activities and tools. *Macmillan International Higher Education*, *10*, 140–152.

Chan, Z. C., Fung, Y. L. and Chien, W. T. (2013). Bracketing in phenomenology: Only undertaken in the data collection and analysis process. *The qualitative report*, *18*(30), 1–9.

Cheah, S. L., Yang, Y. and Saritas, O. (2019). Reinventing product-service systems: the case of Singapore, *Foresight*, *21*(3), 332–361.

Curaj, A. (2010). The For-Uni Blueprint: A Blueprint for Organizing Foresight in Universities, The Publishing House of the Romanian Academy, Bucharest.

Daim, T.U., Chiavetta, D., Porter, A.L. and Saritas, O. (eds.) (2016). Anticipating Future Innovation Pathways through Large Data Analysis, Springer Verlag, Berlin.

Ena, O, Mikova, N., Saritas, O. and Sokolov, A. (2016). A technology trend monitoring methodology: the case of semantic technologies, *Scientometrics*, vol. 103, issue 3, pp. 1013–1041.

Fink, A. (2019). *Conducting research literature reviews: From the internet to paper*. Sage publications.

Grimaldi, M., Cricelli, L., Di Giovanni, M. and Rogo, F. (2014). The patent portfolio value analysis: A new framework to leverage patent information for strategic technology planning. Technological forecasting and social change, *94*, 286–302.

Hung, C. Y., Lee, W. Y. and Wang, D. S. (2013). Strategic foresight using a modified Delphi with end-user participation: A case study of the iPad's impact on Taiwan's PC ecosystem. *Technological Forecasting and Social Change*, *80*(3), 485–497.

Kayser, V. and Blind, K. (2017). Extending the knowledge base of foresight: The contribution of text mining. *Technological Forecasting and Social Change*, *116*, 208–215.

https://doi.org/10.1515/9783110672916-009

Lee, S., Yeo, S. G., Kang, S. J., Han, S. Y., & Lee, S. W. (2015). A Delphi Study on National Public Vaccine Research and Development Policy in Korea. *Health Policy Management, 25*(2), 140.

Lienert, J., Schnetzer, F. and Ingold, K. (2013). Stakeholder analysis combined with social network analysis provides fine-grained insights into water infrastructure planning processes. *Journal of environmental management, 125*, 134–148.

Lummus, R. R., Vokurka, R. J. and Duclos, L. K. (2005). Delphi study on supply chain flexibility. *International journal of production research, 43*(13), 2687–2708.

Miles, I. and Keenan, M. (2002). *Practical Guide to Regional Foresight in the UK*, Publications of the European Communities, Luxembourg.

Miles, I., Saritas, O. and Sokolov, A. (2016). Foresight for Science, Technology and Innovation, Springer Verlag, Berlin.

Mundy, L. (2017). Platelet-rich plasma: a case study for the identification of disinvestment opportunities using horizon scanning. *Australian Health Review, 41*(1), 33–37.

Nugroho, Y. and Saritas, O. (2009). Incorporating network perspectives in Foresight: A methodological proposal, *Foresight*, 11, 6, 21–41.

Phaal, R. and Muller, G. (2009). An architectural framework for roadmapping: Towards visual strategy. *Technological Forecasting and Social Change, 76*(1), 39–49.

Saritas, O. (2006). Systems Thinking for Foresight, Ph.D. Thesis, The University of Manchester, Manchester, UK.

Saritas, O. (2010a). Towards a Systemic Foresight Methodology (SFM), *Foresight, 12*(1), 1.

Saritas, O. (2010b). Systemic Foresight Methodology, The For-Uni Blueprint: A Blueprint for Organizing Foresight in Universities, ed. A. Curaj The Publishing House of the Romanian Academy, Bucharest, 21–31.

Saritas, O. (2013). Systemic Foresight Methodology, in Science, Technology and Innovation Policy for the Future: Potentials and Limits of Foresight Studies, D. Meissner, L. Gokhberg, and A. Sokolov and eds. Springer Verlag, Berlin, 83–117.

Saritas, O. (2020). Foresight in Transition, *Foresight*, forthcoming.

Saritas, O. and Burmaoglu, S. (2015). The evolution of the use of Foresight methods: a scientometric analysis of global FTA research output, *Scientometrics, 105*(1), 497–508.

Saritas, O. and Burmaoglu, S. (2016). Future of sustainable military operations under emerging energy and security considerations, *Technological Forecasting & Social Change, 102*, 331–343.

Saritas, O. and Kuzminov, I. (2017). Global challenges and trends in agriculture: impacts on Russia and possible strategies for adaptation, *Foresight*, (in special issue: Sectoral STI Foresight in Russia, Guest edited by T. Thurner), *19*(2), 218–250.

Saritas, O. and Nugroho, Y. (2012). Mapping issues and envisaging futures: An evolutionary scenario approach, *Technological Forecasting and Social Change, 79*(3), 509–529.

Saritas, O. and Smith, J. (2011). The big picture – trends, wild cards, discontinuities and weak signals, *Futures*, vol. *43*(3), 292–312.

Saul, D. (2019). Domestic military disaster mitigation: A new approach, *Canadian Military Journal, 19*(3), 45–50.

Schoemaker, P. J. (1995). Scenario planning: a tool for strategic thinking. *Sloan management review, 36*(2), 25–50.

Sutherland, W. J., Albon, S. D., Allison, H., Armstrong-Brown, T., et al. (2010). The identification of priority oppertunities for UK nature conservation policy. *Journal of Applied Ecology, 47*, 955–965.

Wulf, T., Meissner, P., Brands, C. and Stubner, S. (2013). Scenario-based strategic planning: A new approach to coping with uncertainty, in Scenario-based strategic planning: Developing strategies in an uncertain world. B. Schwenker, & T. Wulf (eds.). Wiesbaden: Springer gabler, 44–66.

www.ingramcontent.com/pod-product-compliance
Lightning Source LLC
Chambersburg PA
CBHW081109220326

41598CB00038B/7288